Southern Railway Handbook

B. K. COOPER

LONDON

IAN ALLAN LTD

Contents

First published 1983

ISBN 0 7110 1291 1

Published by Ian Allan Ltd, Shepperton, Surrey; and printed by Ian Allan Printing Ltd at their works at Coombelands in Runnymede, England

Front cover: Class D 4-4-0 No 1591 at Hildenborough in July 1939. *Wethersett Collection*

Front cover, inset: The Southern Railway's famous poster of 1925. *Crown Copyright National Railway Museum, York*

Back cover, top: Exterior view of Strood Junction box. *Wethersett Collection*

Back cover, bottom: Class I1x 4-4-2T No 2005 seen near Hurst Green with the 4.15pm Lewes-Victoria in May 1939. *Wethersett Collection*

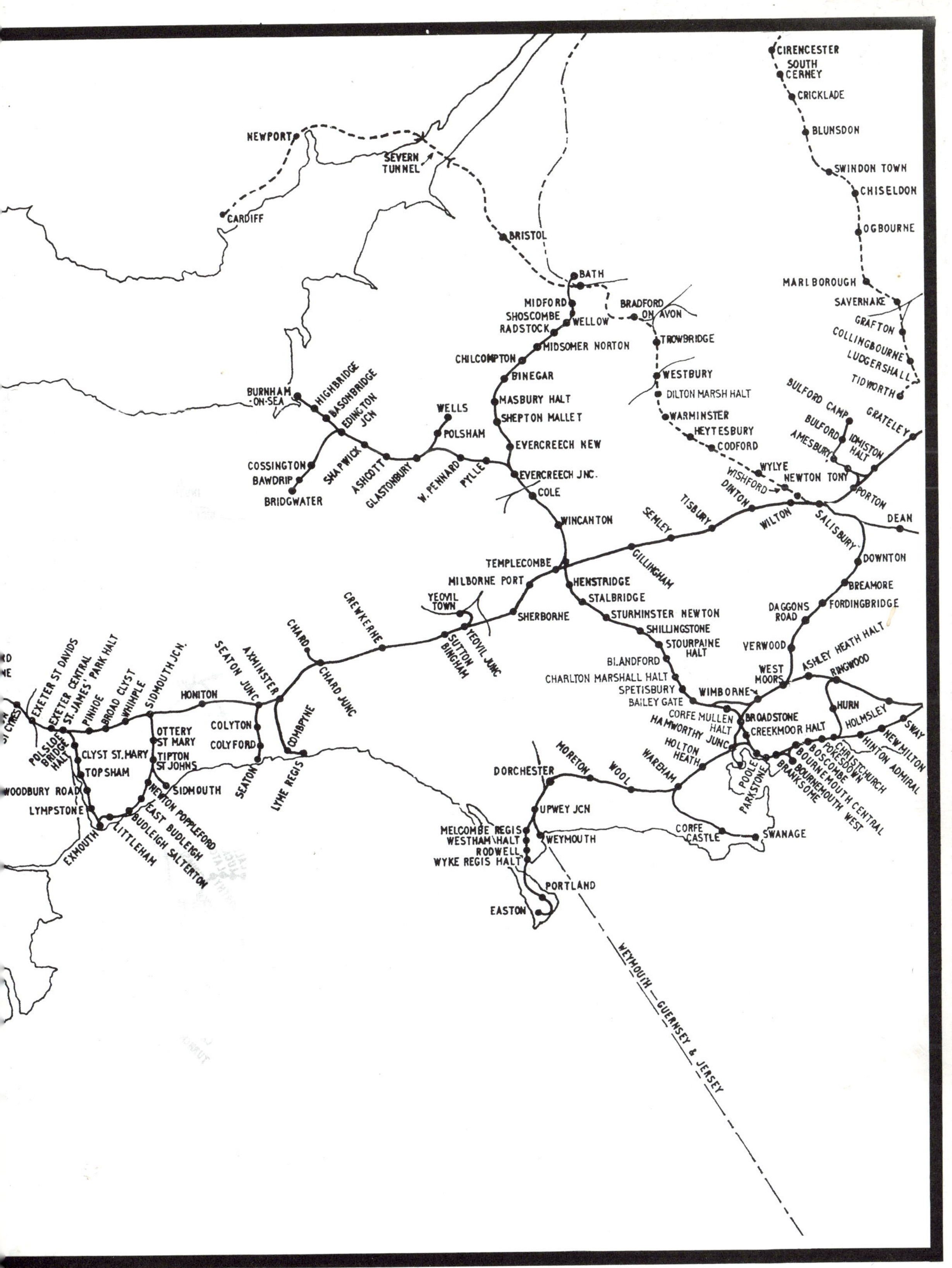

NEWPORT
SEVERN TUNNEL
CARDIFF
BRISTOL
BATH
CIRENCESTER
SOUTH CERNEY
CRICKLADE
BLUNSDON
SWINDON TOWN
CHISELDON
OGBOURNE
MARLBOROUGH
SAVERNAKE
GRAFTON
COLLINGBOURNE
LUDGERSHALL
TIDWORTH
MIDFORD
SHOSCOMBE
WELLOW
RADSTOCK
MIDSOMER NORTON
CHILCOMPTON
BINEGAR
MASBURY HALT
SHEPTON MALLET
EVERCREECH NEW
EVERCREECH JNC.
COLE
WINCANTON
BRADFORD ON AVON
TROWBRIDGE
WESTBURY
DILTON MARSH HALT
WARMINSTER
HEYTESBURY
CODFORD
WYLYE
WISHFORD
NEWTON TONY
BULFORD CAMP
BULFORD
IDMISTON HALT
AMESBURY
GRATELEY
PORTON
DEAN
SALISBURY
WILTON
DINTON
TISBURY
SEMLEY
GILLINGHAM
BURNHAM-ON-SEA
HIGHBRIDGE
BASONBRIDGE
EDINGTON JCN
WELLS
POLSHAM
COSSINGTON
BAWDRIP
BRIDGWATER
SHAPWICK
ASHCOTT
GLASTONBURY
W. PENNARD
PYLLE
TEMPLECOMBE
MILBORNE PORT
HENSTRIDGE
STALBRIDGE
STURMINSTER NEWTON
SHILLINGSTONE
STOURPAINE HALT
BLANDFORD
CHARLTON MARSHALL HALT
SPETISBURY
BAILEY GATE
WIMBORNE
CORFE MULLEN HALT
HAMWORTHY JUNC
HOLTON HEATH
BROADSTONE
CREEKMOOR HALT
DOWNTON
BREAMORE
FORDINGBRIDGE
DAGGONS ROAD
VERWOOD
WEST MOORS
ASHLEY HEATH HALT
RINGWOOD
HURN
HOLMSLEY
SWAY
NEW MILTON
HINTON ADMIRAL
CHRISTCHURCH
POKESDOWN
BOSCOMBE
BOURNEMOUTH CENTRAL
BOURNEMOUTH WEST
BRANKSOME
PARKSTONE
POOLE
YEOVIL TOWN
YEOVIL JUNC
SHERBORNE
SUTTON BINGHAM
CREWKERNE
CHARD
CHARD JUNC
AXMINSTER
SEATON JUNC
HONITON
SIDMOUTH JCN.
COLYTON
COLYFORD
SEATON
COMBPYNE
LYME REGIS
OTTERY ST MARY
TIPTON ST JOHNS
SIDMOUTH
NEWTON POPPLEFORD
EAST BUDLEIGH
BUDLEIGH SALTERTON
LITTLEHAM
EXMOUTH
LYMPSTONE
WOODBURY ROAD
TOPSHAM
CLYST ST. MARY
POLSLOE BRIDGE HALT
EXETER ST DAVIDS
EXETER CENTRAL
ST. JAMES' PARK HALT
PINHOE
BROAD CLYST
WHIMPLE
DORCHESTER
MORETON
WOOL
WAREHAM
CORFE CASTLE
SWANAGE
UPWEY JCN
MELCOMBE REGIS
WESTHAM HALT
RODWELL
WYKE REGIS HALT
WEYMOUTH
PORTLAND
EASTON
WEYMOUTH — GUERNSEY & JERSEY

Preface

The Great Western branch I knew as a boy ended among the Blackdown Hills. Traffic by rail and road moved mainly westward along the river valley towards Tiverton and Exeter. Going south, some very winding roads struggled up and down steep hills, crossed a lonely plateau destined in later years to become a US Air Force base, and emerged after some eight miles at Honiton. This was a New World. Reaching its borders after much effort on the bicycle, I knew exactly how Keats felt on first looking into Chapman's Homer. He compared his emotions with those of an astronomer watching a new planet 'swim into his ken', and I experienced much the same awe and wonder in beholding for the first time a Urie 4-6-0. Familiarity had made the Great Western dull and predictable. The Southern had the fascination of the hitherto unknown.

In later years I marvelled at the complexity of the London suburban network. Main lines on maps of that area were almost indistinguishable from the rest. The effect was like a tangled skein of wool from which a few separate strands emerge after it has been shaken vigorously. I visited the Continent via the Short Sea Routes, anxiously clutching books of tickets authorising me to travel to various destinations via Basle or via Delle.

Living north of the Thames, my opportunities for seeing the Southern except at holiday times were at first rare, but became more numerous when I bought a car for £50 and in the course of my perambulations discovered the footpath at the top of the cutting near Weybridge, which charmed me even more than my local footpath commanding a view of Bushey troughs. But the lines to Sussex and the Kent coast were outside my orbit. I knew them later when 'Southern Railway' was on the point of giving place to 'Southern Region'.

There is a common phrase today: 'tell it like it was'. I envy those meticulous observers who made notes of all they saw and heard, and can obey the instruction in detail. In this book I have included a bibliography in recognition of their work and of my indebtedness to them. I have also had frequent recourse to the Public Records Office at Kew where old Southern timetables and documents are summoned by computer from the sepulchres in which they sleep and for a sympathetic reader recreate the world to which they once belonged.

Comparative trivia put most of the colour into my memories of the Southern Railway. I recall in particular a morning in an office overlooking the concourse at Waterloo. Sounds of departure came faintly to us, and through the windows there was a glimpse of brown and cream Pullmans receding on their way to Bournemouth. The Southern Railway officer who was addressing us broke off to draw our attention to the sight, and in tones of mingled pride and reverence exclaimed 'There goes the Belle'. There must have been something special about the Southern.

B. K. Cooper
Stoneleigh, Surrey
July 1982

1 Origins

All four railway Groups formed by the Railways Act of 1921 had long and distinguished histories. The London & North Eastern was about to celebrate the centenary of the Stockton & Darlington Railway; the London, Midland & Scottish could claim direct descent from the Liverpool & Manchester; and the Great Western was justly proud of retaining a name that had remained unchanged since 1835. The beginnings of these Groups were landmarks in the railway panorama, as widely familiar as the Battle of Hastings or the Spanish Armada in the perspective of history.

The Southern Railway could claim origins of equally respectable age although less generally known. Among the railways that formed the Southern group was the London, Brighton & South Coast, which had begun life as the London & Brighton Railway. In building its line to the coast the London & Brighton absorbed part of the route of the Croydon, Merstham & Godstone Railway. This ancient undertaking, opened on 24 July 1805, was an extension of the slightly older Surrey Iron Railway. Both lines were built for freight alone and worked their traffic with horses. The Croydon, Merstham & Godstone (which never got beyond Merstham) was closed in 1838. Its purchase by the London & Brighton had already been authorised in that company's Act of 15 July 1837 and took effect by the end of 1838, thus cementing a genuine antique into the foundations of the Southern Railway.

Two other forefathers of the Southern Railway are remembered for being first in their particular fields. The Canterbury & Whitstable Railway was the first by a few months to haul passengers with a steam locomotive, and the London & Greenwich was the first railway in London.

When the 150th anniversary of public passenger transport on a steam railway was celebrated in 1980, Canterbury and Whitstable joined in with exhibitions and other events drawing attention to the fact that their venture into steam had begun on 3 May 1830, over four months before the more publicised opening of the Liverpool & Manchester Railway and at a time when passenger trains on the Stockton & Darlington were still horse-drawn. But the C&W's locomotive *Invicta* did not earn the laurels of Stephenson's *Rocket*. The line had steep gradients at both ends and *Invicta* was restricted at first to working between Whitstable and the Canterbury end of a level section 1 mile 330yd long, the rest of the line being cable-worked. The gradients out of Whitstable, steepening to 1 in 50 and 1 in 57, soon proved too much for the locomotive, which was then confined to the level section and another stationary engine was installed for hauling trains from Whitstable station to the top of the bank.

The Canterbury & Whitstable was Canterbury's only railway until the South Eastern's line from Ashford to Ramsgate was opened to Canterbury on 6 February 1846. A connection was put in so that Canterbury & Whitstable trains could use the South Eastern's Canterbury station (now Canterbury West). Whitstable did not acquire a second station until

1
Stone sleepers of the Croydon, Merstham & Godstone Railway discovered during construction of the M25.
John Kay — Photography

2
Opening day on the Canterbury & Whitstable Railway, 3 May 1830. *BR*

1 August 1860 when a line from Faversham to Margate reached the town. The new station was called Whitstable Town to distinguish it from the C&W's Whitstable Harbour. Passenger trains ran over the old Canterbury & Whitstable line right into Southern Railway days, not being withdrawn until the end of 1930. Freight traffic continued for over 20 years more but ceased in 1952. Whitstable Town (now simply Whitstable) and Canterbury West stations are still with us, but there is now no direct railway line between the two places.

The London & Greenwich Railway was opened from a terminus near London Bridge to Deptford on 14 December 1836. It hoped to become the one rail highway into London from the south and this idea was looked on with approval by Parliament, so that at one time the trains of three other companies shared London & Greenwich tracks between the terminus and a point about $1\frac{3}{4}$ miles outside. This was rationalisation, mid-19th century style, and in strong contrast with the maze of lines leading into London which the Southern Railway later inherited. Although the London & Greenwich was leased to the South Eastern Railway in 1845, the company retained its corporate identity until it was merged with the Southern Railway in 1923.

Under the Railways Act 1921 the larger railways in each group were called 'constituent companies' and the smaller ones 'subsidiary companies'. The Southern Railway comprised 5 constituent and 14 subsidiary companies. The constituent companies were:

London & South Western
London, Brighton & South Coast
South Eastern
London, Chatham & Dover
South Eastern & Chatham

3
The Canterbury & Whitstable's steam locomotive *Invicta*. *LPC/IAL*

Strictly speaking there were only four constituent *companies* for the South Eastern & Chatham was a joint committee set up on 5 August 1899 for the joint management of the previously independent and once fiercely competitive London Chatham & Dover and South Eastern Railways.

The list of 14 subsidiary companies was largely made up of names long submerged in the identities of the major railways which had operated their various undertakings. They were as follows:

Bridgwater Railway Company
Brighton & Dyke Railway Company
Freshwater, Yarmouth & Newport (Isle of Wight) Railway Company
Hayling Railway Company
Isle of Wight Central Railway Company
Isle of Wight Railway Company
Lee-on-Solent Railway Company
London & Greenwich Railway Company
Mid Kent Railway Company
North Cornwall Railway Company
Plymouth & Dartmoor Railway Company
Plymouth Devonport & South Western Junction Railway Company
Sidmouth Railway Company
Victoria Station & Pimlico Railway Company

The Plymouth, Devonport & South Western Junction had been absorbed by the LSWR just prior to the formation of the Southern Railway. It was important in that its line from Lydford to Devonport via Tavistock and Bere Alston provided the LSWR with its final approach to Plymouth. Until this route was opened in 1890 the South Western had reached Plymouth from Lydford over the South Devon Railway (later GWR). The PDSWJ also worked the branch from Bere Alston to Callington and Calstock from 1908, having extended the original Callington & Calstock section of the East Cornwall Mineral Railway to Bere Alston, equipping the whole line for passenger traffic.

In 1923 the Southern Railway obtained powers to acquire the Lynton & Barnstaple Railway (1ft $11\frac{1}{2}$in gauge), and in the same year powers were granted for the Somerset & Dorset Railway, previously a leased line, to be transferred jointly to the Southern and the London, Midland & Scottish companies. These lines were not covered by the 1921 Amalgamation of Railways Act which excluded narrow-gauge and jointly-owned railways.

Detailed histories of the companies forming the Southern Railway are listed in the bibliography at the end of this book. The following pages trace the development of the five main constituents in outline.

LONDON & SOUTH WESTERN RAILWAY

Logically the history of the London & South Western Railway should begin with the opening of the first section of the London & Southampton Railway from Nine Elms to Woking Common on 21 May 1838. London & Southampton was a short-lived title, for in 1839 the railway obtained powers to change its name to London & South Western. In 1845 it took over the

4
Waterloo station and engine house, 1848. *BR*

little Bodmin & Wadebridge Railway in Cornwall, which had been opened on 4 July 1834, and it is from that date that the London & South Western, and in later years the Western Section of the Southern Railway, liked to trace its history although the Bodmin & Wadebridge line remained isolated from the rest of the LSWR system until 1895.

To return to the main stream, the London & Southampton opened its line throughout on 11 May 1840, but its London terminus remained at Nine Elms until 11 July 1848 when an extension to the first Waterloo station, then called Waterloo Bridge, was opened. In the meantime the company had been engaged in complex negotiations with the Great Western over extensions into the West Country. A line from Southampton to Dorchester had been promoted locally by a Wimborne solicitor named Castleman and in 1845 the LSW was granted powers to lease and operate it, as well as to run trains into Weymouth over the Great Western from Dorchester. The line, opened throughout on 29 July 1847, followed a somewhat tortuous route and was often known as 'Castleman's Corkscrew'. It made a facing junction with the original London & Southampton route about a mile outside Southampton Town (later Southampton Terminus) station. Until 1859 trains continuing past Southampton had to run into and out of Southampton Town but in 1858 a curve to the Dorchester line was put in at Northam Junction and the local station at Blechynden became Southampton West, taking over the through traffic. The present Southampton station is on the same site and Southampton Terminus is closed. The curve at Northam was acute and imposed a speed limit of 15mph on all trains, which was not relaxed until November 1980, when improvements raised the limit to 25mph.

One of the convolutions of Castleman's Corkscrew took it inland through Ringwood between Brockenhurst and Poole. Bournemouth was only a village when the line was planned, but when it developed as a resort a branch was built from Ringwood, opened on 14 March 1870. The later direct route from Brockenhurst to Poole via Bournemouth was not completed until 5 March 1888.

Portsmouth was first served from Waterloo via Bishopstoke (now Eastleigh), Gosport, and a ferry. The LSW opened a branch from Woking to Guildford on 1 May 1845 and this was later extended to Godalming. A contractor, Thomas Brassey, built a railway as a speculation from Godalming to Havant on the London Brighton & South Coast Railway's line to Portsmouth. The South Western agreed to lease it, for although by arrangement with the LBSC they had reached Portsmouth from the west in 1848, the route via Godalming and Havant would reduce the journey from Waterloo by some 20 miles. Expecting trouble from the LBSC, they sent their first train to Havant with a crowd of navvies on board whose role was to deal with any opposition. This came in the effective form of an LBSC locomotive chained to the track in their path at Havant. There was a skirmish, and the South Western train was obliged to withdraw. Legal action followed, reversing the rough-and-ready verdict of the 'Battle of Havant', and the LBSC was instructed to give free passage to the LSW trains, rivals though they were for the London-Portsmouth traffic. It was hard luck on the Brighton line, but a shorter route between London and the great naval base was in the national interest. The Waterloo-Portsmouth service by the new 'Portsmouth Direct' line began on 24 January 1859.

The South Western had no intention of making Weymouth the western limit of its services. Exeter was the goal, with further penetration into Devon and Cornwall in view in association with various lines then being promoted or built. At one time an extension from Dorchester was proposed but was dropped in favour of a slightly easier route from Salisbury, which had been served by a branch leaving the main line near Basingstoke since 1 May 1857. The branch connected at Salisbury with the independent Salisbury & Yeovil Railway (later acquired by the LSWR), and Yeovil became the springboard for the thrust westwards to Exeter. The new line reached Queen Street station, Exeter, on 19 July 1860. In the years that followed branches were built to Exmouth (1861), Seaton (1868), Sidmouth (1874), and Lyme Regis (1903). Queen Street at first was a terminus but on 1 February 1862 it was connected with the South Devon Railway (later GWR) outside St Davids station by a short line that fell sharply towards St Davids with a gradient of 1 in 37. Beyond Exeter, the Exeter & Crediton Railway branched westwards. It was leased by the LSWR in 1862 and was the stem from which the LSWR system branched out in Devon and Cornwall to carry its trains to Ilfracombe (1874), Plymouth (1876), Torrington and Bude (1879), and Padstow (1899). The Padstow line had reached Wadebridge on 1 June 1895, connecting the isolated Bodmin & Wadebridge with the LSW system for the first time.

At the London end of its system the LSWR had a network of suburban and outer suburban routes extending north and south of its main line. Electrification in this area began on 25 October 1915 between Waterloo and East Putney. By the time of Grouping the third rail had reached Shepperton (via Strawberry Hill and Wimbledon), Hampton Court, and Claygate, and had been laid on the Hounslow loop.

Traditionally the heart of the system was Southampton, and here events were moving fast towards the end of the 19th century. The Southampton Dock Company, incorporated in 1836, was having problems

5
Early days on the London & Brighton Railway — a train crosses the Wick Road viaduct on the outskirts of the resort. *Brighton Public Libraries*

in coping with increasing trade at the port. It had received a loan of £250,000 from the LSWR in 1886 but further large capital expenditure was needed. The railway was the only source of extra funds and so in 1891 negotiations were begun for the LSWR to acquire the docks. Parliament approved, and the sale was completed on 1 November 1892. The age of the big ships was approaching. Kipling wrote:

The boat express is waiting your command!
You will find the *Mauretania* at the quay . . .

His lines encapsulate an enduring image of the London & South-Western Railway.

LONDON BRIGHTON & SOUTH COAST RAILWAY

In accordance with the policy of 'one line into London' mentioned earlier in this chapter, the London & Brighton Railway's line began at a junction with the London & Croydon near the present Norwood Junction. The railway to Brighton was opened throughout on 21 September 1841. London & Brighton trains reached London by using the London & Croydon to Corbetts Lane and the London & Greenwich from there. An old print shows Corbetts Lane drowsing in its seclusion $1\frac{3}{4}$ miles from London Bridge while a smocked waggoner leads his horse under the railway arch, cattle graze in the fields, and a train rattles past overhead.

The London & Brighton Act empowered the railway to build a branch from Brighton to Shoreham. This was completed before the main line and opened to traffic on 11 May 1840. It was the first step in a coastal route through Worthing to Chichester and Portsmouth, reached on 14 June 1847. Work was in hand at the same time on a coastal line running eastwards from Brighton to Lewes and St Leonards, opened throughout on 27 June 1846. These developments made the original London & Brighton title too restrictive. When the company amalgamated with the London & Croydon by an Act of 27 July 1846 the name of the combined undertaking was changed to the more descriptive London Brighton & South Coast Railway.

In early London & Brighton days traffic from London for the east coast or west coast lines had to travel via Brighton, which was a terminal station, making it necessary for through trains to reverse. From 2 October 1847, however, trains for the east coast line could by-pass Brighton and run direct to their destination by means of a cut-off line between Wivelsfield on the main line and Lewes. West coast traffic had to pass through Brighton for considerably longer, but on 3 August 1863 the branch from Three

Bridges, on the London main line, to Horsham and Midhurst was connected to the west coast line at Ford by a new line which diverged from the branch at Hardham Junction, near Pulborough. This connection shortened the LBSC route from London to Portsmouth by nearly 10 miles. A branch from Ford to Littlehampton was opened a fortnight later. On 1 June 1864 Bognor was served by a branch leaving the coast line at Barnham Junction. Eastbourne was much earlier in having rail communication, a branch from the east coast line to the resort having been opened on 14 May 1849; and from 1 February 1852 LBSC trains were extended from St Leonards to Hastings over the South Eastern Railway. Trains between London, Hove and Worthing continued to be routed via Brighton until on 1 July 1879 a curve was opened from Preston Park to Hove which by-passed the terminus.

Thoughts of a London terminus further west than London Bridge appear in LBSC reports of the 1850s. When a railway was built from Wandsworth Common (near the present Clapham Junction) on the LSWR to Crystal Palace, with a branch from there to the LBSC at Norwood Junction, there was talk of sending LBSC trains into Waterloo, but the LSWR was not enthusiastic. The same scheme included an extension for freight from Wandsworth Common to Battersea Wharf. In 1858 another company was authorised to build 'a general station near Victoria Street' and a line crossing the Thames to Battersea. The LBSC subscribed half the capital for the project and was entitled to one half of the station site. The other half was used by the London Chatham & Dover Railway. LBSC trains began running into Victoria station via Norwood Junction and Battersea from 1 October 1860. From then on many LBSC services conveyed a portion for each London terminus, but Victoria became predominantly the station for the railway's South Coast pleasure traffic while London Bridge handled the long-distance commuter, who had begun living as far afield from his daily work as Brighton in the early days of the railway.

When the London & Croydon Railway was taken over it had been engaged on building an extension to Epsom. Further construction in LBSC days connected Epsom with Horsham via Dorking, the link being completed on 1 May 1867. The company now had an alternative route out of London for its trains to West Sussex and Portsmouth. The London-Horsham distance was approximately the same as via the Brighton line and Three Bridges but useful relief was afforded to that busy section.

The basic pattern of LBSC main lines was now complete. Train services included Continental boat trains to Newhaven, which was reached by a branch from the east coast line near Lewes opened on 8 December 1847. Pullman cars first appeared on the Brighton line in 1875 and were soon operating in the company's principal trains. They provided the only en route catering service for the LBSC passenger. The company's first all-Pullman train was introduced in December 1881 — ancestor of the celebrated 'Southern Belle' of 1908, best-known of the LBSC's services. Pullman cars and the unusual yellow livery of Stroudley locomotives provided touches of glamour in a pattern of service that was otherwise utilitarian, and often tolerated rather than admired. They are more often remembered than the company's solid contributions to railway history in signalling, and its early venture in electrification with single-phase current.

THE SOUTH EASTERN RAILWAY

For centuries the Dover Road was the traditional highway for travellers between Great Britain and the Continent. If Brighton beckoned the frivolous, Dover was the goal of the merchant and the diplomat, and equally interesting to the railway promoter. The South Eastern Railway bid for the Dover traffic with a main line from Reigate (now Redhill) via Ashford which was opened throughout to the port on 7 February 1844. It also served Folkestone, where the railway had bought the harbour in 1843 and built a branch to serve it. South Eastern trains travelled between Reigate and London Bridge by the London & Brighton/London & Croydon/London & Greenwich route already mentioned. The London & Brighton section was, in fact, a joint undertaking. The South Eastern had proposed an independent route into London but this would have been parallel with the Brighton line and Parliament advised that 'by the abandonment of the parallel part of the line of the said South Eastern Railway much expenditure of money and much intersection of the country might very advantageously be avoided'. This advice was accepted, the South Eastern making itself responsible for building the section from Reigate to Coulsdon.

In 1843 the South Eastern and London & Croydon Railways had obtained powers to build a branch to a new London terminus at Bricklayers Arms. It left the London & Croydon just before the junction with the London & Greenwich, avoiding the approach to London Bridge over London & Greenwich tracks, for which a toll was payable. The Bricklayers Arms station was opened in May 1844 but its use for passenger trains was discontinued in 1866. It remained in use as a goods depot. The branch also gave access to the LBSC's Willow Walk goods depot adjoining Bricklayers Arms.

Continental traffic was important to the South Eastern from the first. Even when the line was only open to Ashford an SER timesheet drew attention to Boulogne, Calais and Ostend packets reaching Dover in time for passengers to be conveyed to Ashford by coach and there catch the last train to London.

Branches from the Dover line were opened from Maidstone Road (later Paddock Wood) to Maidstone on 25 September 1844; and from Tonbridge to Tunbridge Wells on 20 September 1845. The company then struck out for the North Kent coast with a line from Ashford to Ramsgate and Margate via Canterbury, opened throughout on 1 December 1846. A branch from this route at Minster reached Deal on 1 July 1847.

An incursion into North Kent nearer London followed. The SER had leased the London & Greenwich from the end of 1845. In the same year it was authorised to build the North Kent line from a junction with the London & Greenwich west of Deptford (North Kent East junction) to Gravesend and Strood, completed on 30 July 1849. A line was opened from Maidstone to Strood on 18 June 1856. An extension of the old London & Greenwich line to join the North Kent at Charlton was suspended because of fears that the railway would interfere with the instruments at Greenwich Observatory, and Greenwich remained a terminus until the connection was made on 1 February 1878.

The SER did not intend to leave the LBSC with the monopoly of the Sussex coast. It penetrated to Hastings via Ashford on 13 February 1851, and on 1 February 1852 opened an extension to Hastings of its Tunbridge Wells branch, providing a more direct route to the resort for its own trains and one much shorter than that of the LBSC.

Like the LBSC, the South Eastern looked for a West End terminus. Its ambition was achieved on 11 January 1864 with the opening of Charing Cross station to local trains. Main line services followed on 1 May of the same year. The new terminus was reached by an extension from London Bridge, crossing the Thames on Hungerford Bridge. It was a short but very costly line, partly because in order to use one-sixth of an acre of the grounds of St Thomas's Hospital the railway was obliged to purchase the whole site and buildings. The work also provided the SER with a new city terminus at Cannon Street, reached by a branch from the Charing Cross extension immediately west of London Bridge station and involving the building of another railway bridge across the Thames.

It remains to record two events which filled in the essentials of the SER system as it was acquired by the Southern Railway. One was the line from Redhill to Reading (using two sections of LSWR track), which was completed in August 1849. Connected later with the GWR at Reading, this apparently anomalous penetration into Berkshire by a railway so closely associated with Kent provided a valuable cross-country link between the Midlands and North, the Channel ports, and the resorts of the south-east.

6
The first swing bridge at Folkestone Harbour on the SER branch. *BR*

7
The first station in Maidstone, opened on 30 September 1844 as terminus of the SER branch from Maidstone Road (now Paddock Wood). *BR*

The second development came in May 1868 when a new line was opened from New Cross on the North Kent line to Tonbridge via Chislehurst and Sevenoaks, by-passing the original route through Redhill and thenceforward forming part of the company's main line between Charing Cross and Dover.

LONDON CHATHAM & DOVER RAILWAY

When a railway called the East Kent opened a line from Strood to Canterbury on 9 July 1860 the South Eastern viewed the enterprise as a useful feeder to its own system, and does not seem to have been greatly disturbed when the East Kent obtained powers to extend to Dover, where it arrived in 1861. In the meantime, however, the East Kent had shown its hand by seeking authority for entry to London. In the same year as the Dover line was completed the company extended westwards from Strood to St Mary Cray. In collaboration with the Mid-Kent Railway, it had already linked St Mary Cray by rail with Shortlands, connecting there with an eastward extension of the West End of London & Crystal Palace line, which led to the Victoria Station & Pimlico. From 1 December 1860 LC&D trains reached Victoria by this route, sharing the LBSC side of Victoria until their own adjacent station was ready on 1 July 1862.

On 1 July 1863 the LCDR opened a cut-off from Penge Junction direct to Stewarts Lane Junction on the Victoria Station & Pimlico. LCDR and LBSC trains bound for Victoria shared the same tracks from Stewarts Lane, resulting in considerable congestion on the approaches to the terminus at times. Both railways therefore built separate high level lines on viaduct which crossed over the LSWR main line to Waterloo near Queens Road (now Queenstown Road) station. They were opened in 1867. The earlier low-level tracks passed under the LSWR. In Southern Railway days they were used for freight and for locomotive movements to and from Stewarts Lane mpd, while forming a useful alternative route for use in emergencies.

The Act that empowered the LCDR to enter London also authorised a branch to the City from Herne Hill which crossed the Thames at Blackfriars and joined the Metropolitan Railway near Farringdon Street station. The connection was made on 1 January 1866. A City terminus for trains not proceeding to the Metropolitan line was opened at Holborn Viaduct on 2 March 1874.

Perhaps the LCDR and SER are best remembered for their competition over Continental traffic, but the LCDR was also an important holiday line serving resorts along the North Kent Coast. It had originally turned inland at Faversham to reach Dover, but in

October 1863 a coastal line was completed from Faversham to Margate and Ramsgate via Whitstable, Herne Bay and Birchington-on-Sea. Deal was already served by an SER branch from Minster but a new line from the south, leaving the LCDR near that company's Dover station, was opened in 1874. In 1881 a short loop was put in at the junction to enable trains from the London direction to join the Deal line without entering Dover and reversing.

The company had also been active in the Weald of Kent. Between 1874 and 1 July 1884 it penetrated from Swanley to Ashford. This adventure was strongly opposed by the SER but in later years it provided a valuable alternative route for boat trains, relieving the SER main line to Dover and Folkestone via Tonbridge at times of heavy traffic.

As the years passed it became apparent that the LCDR and the SER could find common interests, and that continuous conflict would be in the interests of neither company. A working partnership was therefore agreed and became effective on 1 January 1899. From that date the two systems were operated by the South Eastern & Chatham Joint Committee. Both railways by this time had taken the form in which they would later be absorbed into the Southern Railway, but some important modifications were made under the joint management committee before all railways passed under Government control in World War 1. Notable among them were the connections put in in 1902/04 between the SER and LCDR London-Dover lines where they crossed near Bickley (Fig 1); and the opening of Dover Marine station for the Continental traffic of both routes in December 1914. It was a period of heavy capital expenditure on improvements to a system which had not enjoyed a favourable public image. Few can have foreseen when the work of putting a somewhat shaky house in order was undertaken that the nation as a whole would be indebted to the South Eastern & Chatham in the years from 1914 to 1918 when it bore so heavy a load of wartime traffic.

Fig 1
Interconnections near Bickley between the main lines to Dover

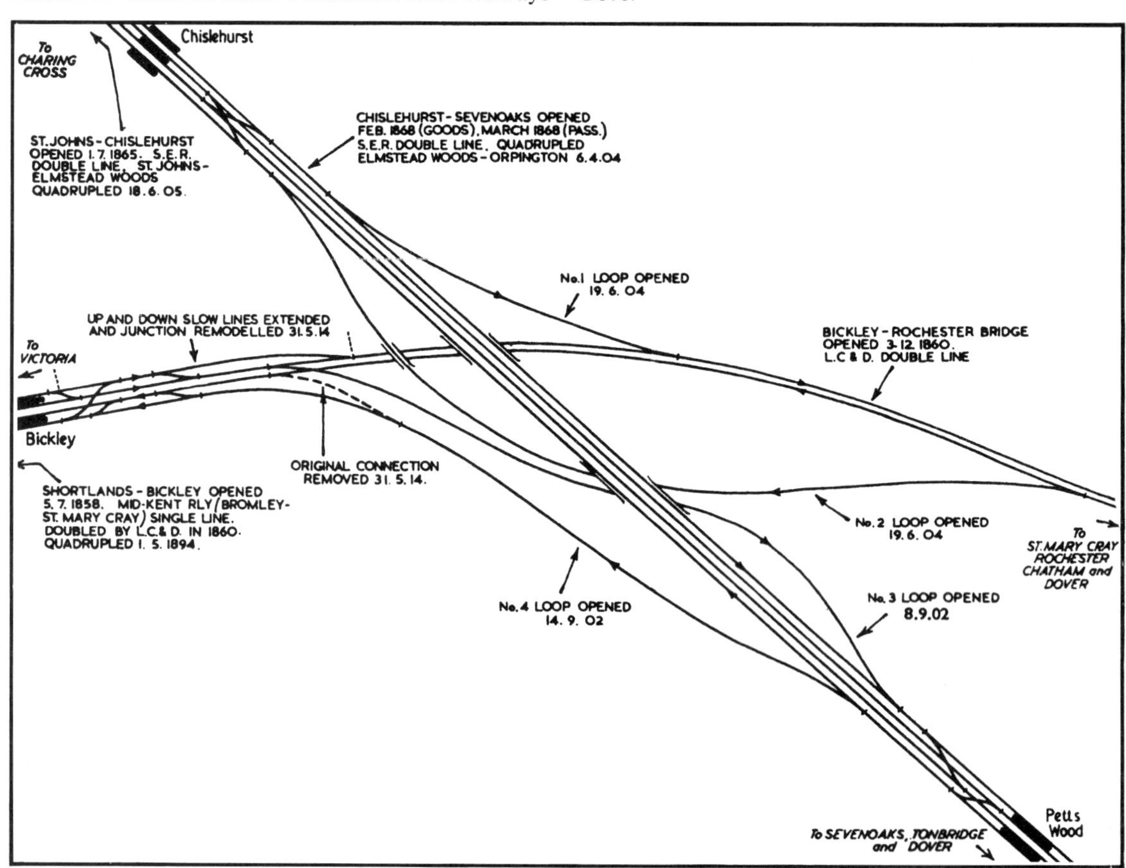

2 Southern Locomotives

On its formation on 1 January 1923 the Southern Railway inherited a stock of 2,281 locomotives from its constituents. The company's Chief Mechanical Engineer was R. E. L. Maunsell, who had held a similar post with the South Eastern & Chatham since 1913. Table 1 shows the locomotive classes and the number of engines in each. Some of them had only a short life under the Southern. The surviving 4-2-2-0 four-cylinder divided-drive locomotives of Drummond's design had gone by 1927. More enduring were the 0-4-2 tender engines — the Adams 'Jubilees' and Stroudley's 'Gladstones'. The last 'Gladstone' went in

Table 1 — Locomotives inherited by the Southern Railway

Wheel arrangement	*Pre-Group Company*	*Year introduced*	*Class*	*CME or builder*	*No of engines in class*
0-4-0T	LSWR	1891	B4	Adams	20
0-4-0T	LSWR	1908	K14	Drummond	5
0-4-0T	LSWR	1913(a)	C14	Drummond	3
0-4-2T	LBSC	1873	D1	Stroudley	107
0-4-2T	LBSC	1910	D1x	Stroudley	1
0-4-4T	LCDR	1884	A	Kirtley	18
0-4-4T	LCDR	1884	A1	Kirtley	12
0-4-4T	LCDR	1884	A2	Kirtley	6
0-4-4T	LBSC	1892	D3	R. Billinton	2
0-4-4T	LBSCR	1909	D3x	R. Billinton	34
0-4-4T	LSWR	1888	F6	Adams	30
0-4-4T	LSWR	1888	T1	Adams	20
0-4-4T	SECR	1904	H	Wainwright	66
0-4-4T	LSWR	1897	M7	Drummond	55
0-4-4T	LSWR	1897	X14	Drummond	50
0-4-4T	LSWR	1889	O2	Adams	60
0-4-4T	SER	1881	Q	Stirling	32
0-4-4T	SECR	1903	Q1	Wainwright	46
0-4-4T	LCDR	1891	R	Kirtley	18
0-4-4T	SECR	1900	R1	Wainwright	15
0-6-0T	LBSCR	1872	A1	Stroudley	7
0-6-0T	LBSCR	1872	A1x	Stroudley	15
0-6-0T	LBSCR	1874	E1	Stroudley	61
0-6-0T	LBSCR	1911	E1x	L. Billinton	1
0-6-0T	LBSCR	1913	E2	L. Billinton	10
0-6-0T	LSWR	1894	G6	Adams	34
0-6-0T	SECR	1909	P	Wainwright	8
0-6-0T	SER	1888	R	Stirling	11
0-6-0T	SECR	1910	R1	Wainwright	13
0-6-0T	LCDR	1879	T	Kirtley	10
0-6-0T	Freshwater, Yarmouth & Newport	1876		Stroudley	1(b)

Wheel arrangement	*Pre-Group Company*	*Year introduced*	*Class*	*CME or builder*	*No of engines in class*
0-6-0T	IoW Central	1872		Stroudley	4(b)
0-6-0T	LSWR	1907		Hawthorn, Leslie	1(c)
0-6-0ST	SECR	1917	S(d)	Maunsell	1
0-6-0ST	LSWR	1876	0330	Beattie	20
0-6-0ST	Freshwater, Yarmouth & Newport	1902		Manning, Wardle	1
0-6-2T	LBSC	1891	E3	R. Billinton	17
0-6-2T	LBSC	1897	E4	R. Billinton	70
0-6-2T	LBSC	1909	E4x	R. Billinton	4
0-6-2T	LBSC	1902	E5	R. Billinton	26
0-6-2T	LBSC	1911	E5x	R. Billinton	4
0-6-2T	LBSC	1904	E6	R. Billinton	10
0-6-2T	LBSC	1911	E6x	R. Billinton	2
0-6-2T	LSWR	1907	—	Hawthorn Leslie	2(c)
2-4-0T	Isle of Wight Railway	1864	—	Beyer, Peacock	7
2-4-0T	Isle of Wight Central	1876	—	Beyer, Peacock	4
2-4-0WT	LSWR	1874	0329	Beattie	3
4-2-4T	LSWR	1899	F9	Drummond	1(e)
4-4-0T	Isle of Wight Central	1890	—	Black, Hawthorn	1
2-4-2T	Lynton & Barnstaple	1900	—	Baldwin	1(f)
2-6-2T	Lynton & Barnstaple	1897	—	Manning, Wardle	3(f)
2-6-4T	SECR	1917	K	Maunsell	1
4-4-2T	LBSC	1906	I1/I1x	Marsh	20
4-4-2T	LBSC	1907	I2	Marsh	10
4-4-2T	LBSC	1907	I3	Marsh	27
4-4-2T	LBSC	1908	I4	Marsh	5
4-4-2T	LSWR	1883	046	Adams	7(g)
4-4-2T	LSWR	1882	0415	Adams	48
4-6-2T	LSWR	1921	H16	Urie	5
4-6-2T	LBSC	1910	J1	Marsh	1
4-6-2T	LBSC	1912	J2	Marsh	1
4-8-0T	LSWR	1921	G16	Urie	4
0-4-2	LSWR	1887	A12/04	Adams	90
0-4-2	LBSC	1882	B1	Stroudley	26
4-4-0	SER	1898	B	Stirling	4
4-4-0	SER	1910	B1	Stirling	25
4-4-0	LBSC	1895	B2x	Marsh	25
4-4-0	LBSC	1899	B4	R. Billinton	31
4-4-0	LBSC	1922	B4x	R. Billinton	2
4-4-0	LSWR	1898	C8	Drummond	10
4-4-0	SECR	1901	D	Wainwright	41
4-4-0	SECR	1921	D1	Maunsell	10
4-4-0	LSWR	1912	D15	Drummond	10
4-4-0	SECR	1905	E	Wainwright	15
4-4-0	SECR	1919	E1	Maunsell	11
4-4-0	SECR	1883	F	Stirling	12
4-4-0	SECR	1903	F1	Wainwright	75
4-4-0	SECR	1899	G	Pickersgill	5(h)
4-4-0	LSWR	1901	K10	Drummond	40
4-4-0	SECR	1914	L	Wainwright & Maunsell	22
4-4-0	LSWR	1903	L11	Drummond	40

Wheel arrangement	*Pre-Group Company*	*Year introduced*	*Class*	*CME or builder*	*No of engines in class*
4-4-0	LSWR	1904	L12	Drummond	20
4-4-0	LCDR	1880	M1	Kirtley	1
4-4-0	LCDR	1880	M2	Kirtley	1
4-4-0	LCDR	1880	M3	Kirtley	26
4-4-0	LSWR	1903	S11	Drummond	10
4-4-0	LSWR	1892	T3	Adams	20
4-4-0	LSWR	1895	T6	Adams	10
4-4-0	LSWR	1897	T7	Drummond	1
4-4-0	LSWR	1901	E10	Drummond	5
4-4-0	LSWR	1899	T9	Drummond	66
4-4-0	LSWR	1890	X2	Adams	20
4-4-0	LSWR	1895	X6	Adams	10
4-4-0	LSWR	1880	0135	Adams	3
4-4-0	LSWR	1879	0380	Adams	8
4-4-0	LSWR	1883	0445	Adams	12
4-4-0	LSWR	1884	0460	Adams	21
4-2-2-0	LSWR	1897	T7	Drummond	1
4-2-2-0	LSWR	1901	E10	Drummond	5
4-4-2	LBSC	1905	H1	Marsh	5
4-4-2	LBSC	1911	H2	Marsh	6
4-6-0	LSWR	1913	H15	Urie	16
4-6-0	LSWR	1908	G14	Drummond	5
4-6-0	LSWR	1918	N15	Urie	20
4-6-0	LSWR	1910	P14	Drummond	5
4-6-0	LSWR	1920	S15	Urie	20
4-6-0	LSWR	1911	T14	Drummond	10
0-6-0	LCDR	1877	B1	Kirtley	2
0-6-0	LCDR	1891	B2	Kirtley	6
0-6-0	SECR	1900	C	Wainwright	108
0-6-0	LBSC	1882	C1	Stroudley	1
0-6-0	LBSC	1893	C2	R. Billinton	24
0-6-0	LBSC	1902	C2x	R. Billinton	31
0-6-0	LBSC	1906	C3	Marsh	10
0-6-0	SER	1878	O	Stirling	31
0-6-0	SER	1903	O1	Wainwright	56
0-6-0	LSWR	1897	700	Drummond	30
0-6-0	LSWR	1872	0273	Beattie	6
0-6-0	LSWR	1874	0302	Beattie	15
0-6-0	LSWR	1881	0395	Adams	20
2-6-0	LBSC	1913	K	L. Billinton	17
2-6-0	SECR	1917/22	N/N1	Maunsell	16
4-6-4T	LBSC	1914	L	L. Billinton	7

Notes:
a Built originally in 1906 as 2-2-0T rail motor engines
b Ex-LBSC 'Terriers'
c Built for Plymouth, Devonport & South Western Junction Railway
d Rebuild of SECR C class 0-6-0
e Inspection saloon
f 2ft gauge
g Built as 4-4-0T, 1879; Rebuilt to 4-4-2T, 1883
h Built by Neilson, Reid for Great North of Scotland Railway to Pickersgill's design but taken over by SECR

8
Maunsell's 'N' class 2-6-0 originated before Grouping and continued to be built by the Southern Railway. No 1403 illustrated was one of the later engines and is seen at Dover in 1935. *O. S. Nock*

1933 but the 'Jubilees' lasted until 1948. Otherwise the wheel arrangements were conventional, although only the LSWR could show 4-6-0s.

Maunsell's time in charge of SECR locomotive affairs had covered the years of World War 1 and saw only two new designs. The first of his 'N' class 2-6-0s came out of Ashford in 1917, followed by 11 more up to 1922. These were two-cylinder engines with 5ft 6in wheels but a three-cylinder version ('N1') followed. Maunsell also produced a 2-6-4T similar to Class N but with 6ft dia wheels for passenger work. This engine was the forerunner of the 'River' class built after Grouping and later converted to 2-6-0 tender engines. More 'N' class 2-6-0s were built in Southern Railway days, some of them at Woolwich under a Government scheme to maintain employment at the arsenal when its wartime activities ended.

The shortage of modern express passenger engines was Maunsell's first preoccupation on the Southern. Heavier rolling stock was being introduced and at the same time management was asking for faster schedules. The Folkestone service was Maunsell's first care. Under the SECR the best trains had made the Charing Cross-Folkestone journey of $69\frac{1}{2}$ miles in 80min non-stop. This was achieved satisfactorily by Wainwright's 'L' class 4-4-0s of 1914 but the introduction of corridor coaches and one intermediate stop in the same schedule called for action. There being no time for a new design, Maunsell redesigned some vital

9
'N1' class three-cylinder 2-6-0 No 878. *LPC/IAL*

10
'L1' class 4-4-0 No 783 carries the 'A' prefix to its number, denoting an Eastern Section locomotive

features of the 'L' class, increasing the valve travel, raising boiler pressure, using smaller cylinders and improving the draughting. All this was done with the maximum possible use of existing components. The new engines with these modifications were built by North British and were classified 'L1'; they enabled the 80min timing to be maintained, including the additional stop, with loads up to 320 tons as compared with the maximum of 225 tons for Class L.

On the LSWR the most recent 4-6-0s were those designed by R. W. Urie. Maunsell again took a short cut to providing more motive power by redesigning the valve gear and blast arrangements of Urie's 'N15' class and put in hand the building of more engines embodying these changes at Eastleigh Works and the North British Locomotive Co Ltd. These 4-6-0s and their successors formed the 74 strong 'King Arthur' class. The names were a public relations masterstroke at a time when the new Group was having a rough passage, its services coming in for much criticism for unreliability and overcrowding. The press was so vociferous, in fact, that the company replied in the principal daily papers of 22 January 1925 with an advertisement recalling the conspicuous part played by its constituents on the home front in the recent war and pointing out the problems of re-equipment. Now the 'King Arthurs' associated the railway in the public mind with the world of chivalry and old romance, hopefully overriding the image of overcrowded trains on wet Monday mornings.

11
'Urie Arthur' 4-6-0 No 453 *King Arthur*. *IAL*

12
'King Arthur' ('N15') class 4-6-0 No 771 *Sir Sagramore*, one of the series built by North British and known as 'Scotch Arthurs'. *IAL*

13
No 804 *Sir Cador of Cornwall* was one of the 'King Arthurs' with six-wheel tenders for service on the Central Section although in this photograph it carries the Western Section 'E' prefix above the number on the tender and the 'A' power classification on the frame next to the buffer beam. *IAL*

14
Class S15 was a variant of the 'King Arthurs' with smaller wheels. No 834 is one of the 15 engines of this class, built at Eastleigh in 1927/8. *IAL/LPC*

15
Maunsell continued building 4-6-0s similar to Urie's 'H15' class. Urie 'H15' No 488 is at Waterloo in Southern Railway livery. *Real Photos*

For many people in those days the 'King Arthurs' *were* the Southern Railway. Its lines carried a high proportion of holiday travellers from all over the country and their only experience of the Southern was probably a journey behind one of this ubiquitous class to a coastal resort or a Channel Port. Although South Western in origin, the 'Arthurs' spread to the SECR lines, and a batch of 14 was built with six-wheel instead of the classic LSWR eight-wheel tenders for working on the Central Section, although electrification soon cut short their career on the LBSC services.

Maunsell also continued the building of Urie's 4-6-0 class of 1914 with 6ft coupled wheels (Class H15), and in 1927 introduced a small-wheeled (5ft 7in) variant of the 'King Arthurs' (Class S15). The 'S15', too, had a Urie progenitor in some LSWR 4-6-0s built in 1920 and 1921. The one 2-6-4 passenger tank engine built by Maunsell just before Grouping was soon joined by others to form Class K, better known as the 'River' class, all being named after English rivers. The last of them was a three-cylinder engine, classified 'K1', with a form of conjugated valve gear for the inside cylinder.

The 'Rivers' were put to work on the Eastern and Central Sections but their career as fast passenger tanks was short. On 27 August 1927 'River' class No 800, *River Cray*, was derailed near Sevenoaks while hauling an express from Cannon Street to Deal, 13 passengers being killed. The Inspecting Officer of the Ministry of Transport concluded that the derailment was caused by the oscillation of the engine, which might have been set up by certain defects in the permanent way. In commenting on the report at the next annual general meeting of the Southern Railway Company the Chairman, General Baring, remarked that measurements had shown the superelevation of one rail on the curve where the accident happened to be slightly out of adjustment in some places and he accepted that this might have been sufficient to set up the oscillation.

The part played by track irregularity was still being debated in the 1930s but it is now the general view that the oscillation was caused by surging of water in the side tanks and that the 'River' design was prone to instability when this occurred. All the class were rebuilt as 2-6-0 tender engines, forming Classes U and U1. More engines of both classes were built. The 'U' class with two cylinders and 'U1' with three, the latter continuing the three-cylinder version represented in the original 'Rivers' by only one locomotive. In Class U1, however, the conjugated gear was dropped in favour of three sets of Walschaerts valve gear.

Meanwhile Maunsell had been engaged on the design of an entirely new 4-6-0 for the heavy Continental trains by this time reaching 500 tons in weight. The first of the class, No 850 *Lord Nelson*, came out in 1926. At this time the express steam locomotive was the most familiar epitome of speed and power to most people, and the four new railway Groups were each anxious to claim that they possessed the most 'powerful' article of this nature. 'Power' was interpreted as tractive effort, which was calculated from a formula. The result was properly qualified as 'nominal' tractive effort but this adjective was usually omitted in publicity material. For a short time *Lord Nelson* was top of the power league with a nominal tractive effort of 33,500lb. It was a four-cylinder locomotive with the drive divided between first and second coupled axles. The distinctive feature of the design was the setting of the cranks to give eight beats per revolution to provide

16
Maunsell built his first 2-6-4 passenger tank for the SECR but added more after Grouping, forming the 'River' class. No 799 *River Test* was one of the post-Grouping engines. *IAL/LPC*

17
The 'Rivers' were rebuilt as 2-6-0 tender engines after the Sevenoaks derailment, forming the nucleus of Class U. No 805 was originally *River Camel*. *IAL/LPC*

a uniform torque and steady draught. Coupled wheel diameter was 6ft 7in.

Various modifications took place in Southern Railway days. Before construction of the last five engines of the class of 16 began, No 859 *Lord Hood* was fitted with 6ft 3in coupled wheels to see if running over the steeply graded sections of the Victoria-Dover line would be improved. No significant difference was found, and although *Lord Hood* retained the smaller wheels until withdrawal the new engines were given the standard 6ft 7in size. The class had a mixed reputation in its early years and it was suggested that the special crank angle might not be giving the advantages hoped for. In 1933 Maunsell changed the angle to the conventional 90° in No 865 *Sir John Hawkins*. Again the results were not convincing enough for the other engines to be altered similarly although *Sir John Hawkins* retained the 90° setting until withdrawn.

In 1934 Maunsell equipped No 862 *Lord Collingwood* with two Kylchap blastpipes and a double chimney. The modification earned the approval of the crews who handled the engine on the heavy Continental expresses although there was an increase in fuel consumption compared with the standard 'Lord Nelson'. However, it was still below that of *Sir John Hawkins* with the 90° crank setting.

In 1937 Maunsell was succeeded by O. V. S. Bulleid. The previous year had seen the introduction of the 'Night Ferry' through sleeping car service between London and Paris, a heavy train which required the services of two 4-4-0s of Classes L1, L or El (another Maunsell rebuild of a Wainwright design) in various combinations. On the other Continental expresses the timekeeping of the 'Lord Nelsons' was moderate. The need for still larger engines was apparent, and to fill the gap before a new design could be produced Bulleid made further experiments with draughting.

Bulleid's first step was taken in 1938 when he equipped No 865 *Sir John Hawkins* with a Kylchap blastpipe, and No 863 *Lord Rodney* with a Lemaître blastpipe and large diameter stovepipe chimney. Trials on boat expresses showed the superiority of the Lemaître equipment, which was fitted to all the 'Lord Nelsons' between November 1938 and October 1939. The large-diameter stovepipe on No 863 had the functional simplicity of a dustbin, with which it was often compared by contemporary observers. Improvements were made in the aesthetics of this accoutrement as fitted to all the engines.

The 'Lord Nelsons' were a response to the needs of the Eastern Section of the Southern Railway but they worked on the Western Section as well, sharing West of England services with the 'King Arthurs' between Waterloo and Salisbury (working to and from Exeter

18
The three-cylinder 'River', No A890, *River Frome*, was classified 'U1' when rebuilt as a 2-6-0. More three-cylinder engines were built, No 1902 belonging to a later batch. *O. J. Morris*

19
An early photograph of 4-6-0 No 850 *Lord Nelson*, described in the caption as 'Britain's most powerful passenger engine' having a tractive effort of 14.96 tons — 'the highest in the country'. *IAL*

20
'Lord Nelson' No 862 *Lord Collingwood* equipped by Maunsell with two Kylchap blastpipes and double chimney. *LPC/IAL*

in their early days), and taking turns with the same class on the Bournemouth line, where their most regular duty up to the war was the 'Bournemouth Belle' Pullman. In the war years they worked increasingly on this route when Service travel and petrol rationing brought heavier traffic to the railway. When the Eastern Section's formidable 'Night Ferry' was below its full load a 'Nelson' might work it unaided but the class usually needed a pilot. Up to the war the 'Night Ferry' remained for the most part a 'two 4-4-0' train.

Having continued the 'Nelson' story into Bulleid's day, it is now necessary to go back to Maunsell and the next problem confronting him. New motive power was needed for increasing loads on the Tonbridge-Hastings line, where severe loading gauge restrictions set special difficulties for the locomotive designer. Mountfield Tunnel, near Battle, had been relined in the 1850s, giving it a smaller cross-section than similar works elsewhere on the South Eastern Railway, and making it necessary to work the line with rolling stock 6in narrower than normal. The dimensions of outside cylinders in a new locomotive would have to be limited for the same reason, which meant that a two-cylinder design of adequate power was impracticable. Six coupled wheels would have been desirable for adhesion, but a shorter engine was preferable for the curvature of the Hastings line as well as being suitable for the existing turntables. Maunsell's choice for these conditions was a three-cylinder 4-4-0.

In his new engines Maunsell made as many parts as possible interchangeable with the 'Lord Nelsons', but this policy could not extend to the boiler, for which the 'Nelson' boiler was too heavy, while a round-topped firebox was needed to allow a good lookout from the cab. Mountfield Tunnel exerted its influence here as well, for its narrow bore made it necessary to taper the cabsides inwards towards the top. The boiler adopted was therefore a shortened version of the 'King Arthur' pattern. The first locomotive of the new series was turned out from Eastleigh in March 1930, launching the celebrated 'Schools' class. Their nominal tractive effort of 25,130lb was the highest of any 4-4-0 built in Great Britain. This was another publicity point for the Southern Railway, but still more effective was the choice of 'school' names which linked the engines firmly with local loyalties. At first it had been intended to limit the choice to schools on the Southern Railway but in the event the range was extended.

In 1930 some work remained to be done between Tonbridge and St Leonards before the line could accept the new engines. The first of them therefore were put to work on other Southern main lines and it was soon apparent that a design largely dictated by a set of unusual local conditions was in fact an all-round winner.

Regular service on the Tonbridge-Hastings line began in July 1931. In the meantime 'Schools' had been working Eastbourne-London trains on the Central Section. They moved on when electrification reached the resort in 1935 and began their better-known association with Waterloo-Portsmouth services. When the 'Portsmouth Direct' line was electrified in 1937 the 'Schools' which had been at Fratton were transferred to Bournemouth, where they earned further laurels. They were equally at home on the old LCDR line to the Kent Coast. Reviewing nine runs with the class from Margate to Victoria in the September 1940 issue of *The Railway Magazine*, Cecil J. Allen commented: 'One notable feature of these runs is the increase in maximum speeds over previous standards; with the 'Schools' the recorder can almost rely, on the up journey, on getting a maximum of 80mph at Farningham Road on the principal expresses, as on all the tabulated runs with one exception. With the ability to keep time over such grades with loads up to nearly 400 tons, also, the "Schools" can claim to have the Kent Coast situation well in hand'.

It was, however, the Bournemouth line in the years immediately before World War 2 that is often considered to have seen the zenith of 'Schools' performance. The engines were used on the 'Bournemouth Limited', non-stop between Waterloo and Bournemouth Central in two hours; and some were painted like the coaches in the light green favoured by Bulleid. The standard Southern green was described as 'sage'. Bulleid preferred mineral to vegetable and chose the shade known as 'malachite' after a carbonate of copper. These were the streamline years, but streamlining for the Southern Railway was still on the drawing board where Bulleid's concept of a new Pacific was taking shape. In February 1938, however, 'Schools' No 935 *Sevenoaks* was fitted with a streamlined plywood casing at Eastleigh Works with the idea of its appearing at the head of the 'Limited' in this modern guise. It was photographed for the records, carrying the temporary number 999, but in this form never made more than a tentative journey to Micheldever and back early one morning. Apparently the casing vibrated violently and it was removed without further experiment.

Before considering Bulleid's distinctive contribution to Southern Railway locomotives three other Maunsell designs must be mentioned. One was the powerful 'Z' class 0-8-0 shunter, eight of which were built at Brighton in 1929. No more were built, because after Maunsell had introduced diesel-electric shunters in 1937 comparative trials showed the superior economy of the diesel.

In 1931 Maunsell's 'W' class 2-6-4T appeared, a three-cylinder engine similar in style to the original 'River' class passenger tanks but with 5ft 6in coupled wheels. This class was particularly identified with cross-London freight workings between Southern Railway yards and those of the companies north of the Thames. These routes abounded in junctions and short, steep gradients. The high tractive effort of 29,452lb from the 'W' class was useful in recovery from signal checks and in hauling trains up the slope to flyovers.

21
Bulleid's modification of No 863 *Lord Rodney* with Lemaître multiple-jet blastpipe and large-diameter stovepipe chimney. *BR*

Maunsell's last design before retirement was the 'Q' class 0-6-0. This was a general freight and secondary passenger duties locomotive with 18 tons axle-load, giving it a wide route-availability so that it could take over work that was still being done by some ageing survivors of the pre-Grouping companies. It was an economical and practical design, making use of existing parts as far as possible. Maunsell retired through ill health before building of the class began and they were seen into service by Bulleid in 1938.

Apart from these new locomotives, Maunsell was responsible for the rebuilding of the LBSC express passenger Baltic tanks as 4-6-0 tender engines in 1934. With electrification of the Brighton and Eastbourne main lines there was little work for these engines to do, for the generous LBSC loading gauge to which they were built restricted their use elsewhere on the Southern system. In the rebuild the boiler pressure was raised from 170 to 180lb/sq in. A new side-window cab and shortened chimney brought the locomotives within the loading gauge of the Southern Railway generally and allowed their use on any of the main lines except Tonbridge-Hastings. The name of the LBSC war memorial engine, *Remembrance*, was retained and the engines were known as the 'Remembrance' class, but the others were named after famous

22
'Z' class 0-8-0 shunting tank No 953. Eight of the class were built in 1929 but in 1937 Maunsell introduced diesel-electric shunters for these duties. *IAL*

23
'Schools' class No 903 at Charing Cross. *LPC/IAL*

24
Maunsell's 'W' class 2-6-4T was intended mainly for heavy freight traffic in the London area. *IAL*

25
'Q' class 0-6-0 No 534, Maunsell's last design which went into service after his retirement. *O. J. Morris*

26
No 2329 *Stephenson* is one of Maunsell's rebuilds of the LBSC Baltic tanks, forming Class N15X. *BR*

engineers of the past, perpetuating the theme begun by the LBSC in 1921 by naming Baltic No 329 *Stephenson.* The 'Remembrance' 4-6-0s were closely equivalent to the 'King Arthurs'.

O. V. S. Bulleid came to the Southern Railway from the LNER, where he had been assistant to Sir Nigel Gresley. On taking charge his study of SR express working led first to the modified exhaust arrangements of the 'Lord Nelsons' which have been noted already. In 1939 be began a similar procedure with the 'Schools', 20 of which received Lemaître blastpipes and large-diameter chimneys up to 1941. No more were modified after that year and those which had not been dealt with by then retained their original blastpipes and chimneys until the end.

Bulleid's survey of Southern steam practice showed him the need for larger express locomotives. His developments of existing classes were to fill the gap until he could provide the railway with its first Pacific. The war might have frustrated his plans, for the building of new express passenger locomotives was banned, but Bulleid had chosen 6ft 2in coupled wheels and argued successfully that his Pacific design was a general-purpose locomotive. The first 'Merchant Navy' 4-6-2 came out in 1941 and immediately emphasised its designer's originality to those who had not been aware of it before. Much has been said about the unconventional valve gear and the 'air-smoothed' exterior (a welcome variant from the overworked 'streamlined' even if the effect was less happy visually). The significant feature of the locomotive was its boiler. Some figures are given in Table 2 but it may be noted here that in comparison with the 'Nelsons' the total heating surface was increased by some 38% and the grate area by 47%, while the pressure of 280lb/sq in was the highest used up to that time in a British express locomotive other than experimental types. Weight problems had been pressing, and the higher pressure gave Bulleid the tractive effort he was looking for with the relatively small cylinder dimensions of 18in by 24in. Two thermic syphons improved water circulation round the firebox. The nominal tractive effort was 37,500lb, an increase of 10.6% over the 'Nelsons'.

The chain drive of the valve gear was an expedient. Bulleid placed the valve gear of all three cylinders between the frames and enclosed it, together with the connecting rod of the inside cylinder, in a casing of

Table 2 — Principal dimensions of locomotives built for the Southern Railway

Wheel arr	*Class*	*Designer*	*Weight Tons Cwt*	*Boiler pressure lb/sq in*	*Cylinders in*	*Driving wheels*	*TE lb*
4-4-0	L1	Maunsell	57 16	180	$20\frac{1}{2}\times26$	6ft 8in	18,910
4-6-0	N15	Urie	77 5	180	21×28	6ft 7in	23,900 (a)
4-6-0	N15	Maunsell	79 18	200	$20\frac{1}{2}\times28$	6ft 7in	25,320 (b)
4-6-0	N15	Maunsell	80 1	200	$20\frac{1}{2}\times28$	6ft 7in	25,320 (c)
4-6-0	N15	Maunsell	80 19	200	$20\frac{1}{2}\times28$	6ft 7in	25,320 (d)
4-6-0	S15	Maunsell	79 5	200	$20\frac{1}{2}\times28$	5ft 7in	29,860
4-6-0	N15X	Maunsell	73 2	180	21×28	6ft 9in	23,300 (e)
4-6-0	'Lord Nelson'	Maunsell	83 10	220	$16\frac{1}{2}\times26$ (4)	6ft 7in	33,500
2-6-0	N	Maunsell	61 4	200	19×28	5ft 6in	26,000
2-6-0	U	Maunsell	62 6	200	19×28	6ft 0in	23,866 (f)
2-6-0	U1	Maunsell	65 6	200	16×28 (3)	6ft 0in	25,387 (g)
4-4-0	V	Maunsell	67 2	220	$16\frac{1}{2}\times26$ (3)	6ft 7in	25,130
4-6-2	'Merchant Navy'	Bulleid	92 10	280	18×24 (3)	6ft 2in	37,500
4-6-2	'West Country'	Bulleid	80 10	280	16×24 (3)	6ft 2in	31,000
0-6-0	Q	Maunsell	49 10	200	19×26	5ft 1in	26,157
0-6-0	Q1	Bulleid	51 5	230	19×26	5ft 1in	30,000
2-6-4T	W	Maunsell	90 14	200	$16\frac{1}{2}\times28$ (3)	5ft 6in	29,452
0-8-0T	Z	Maunsell	71 12	180	16×28 (3)	4ft 8in	29,376

Notes:

a The 'Urie Arthurs', improved by Maunsell and named
b 'Eastleigh Arthurs', built in Southern Railway days
c 'Scotch Arthurs', built by North British
d Built by North British, fitted with 6-wheel tenders
e 'Remembrance' class, rebuilt from LBSC Baltic tanks
f Class includes rebuilt 'River' class 2-6-4Ts
g Includes the rebuilt three-cylinder 'River' 2-6-4T

Fig 2
One set of 'Merchant Navy' chain-driven valve gear

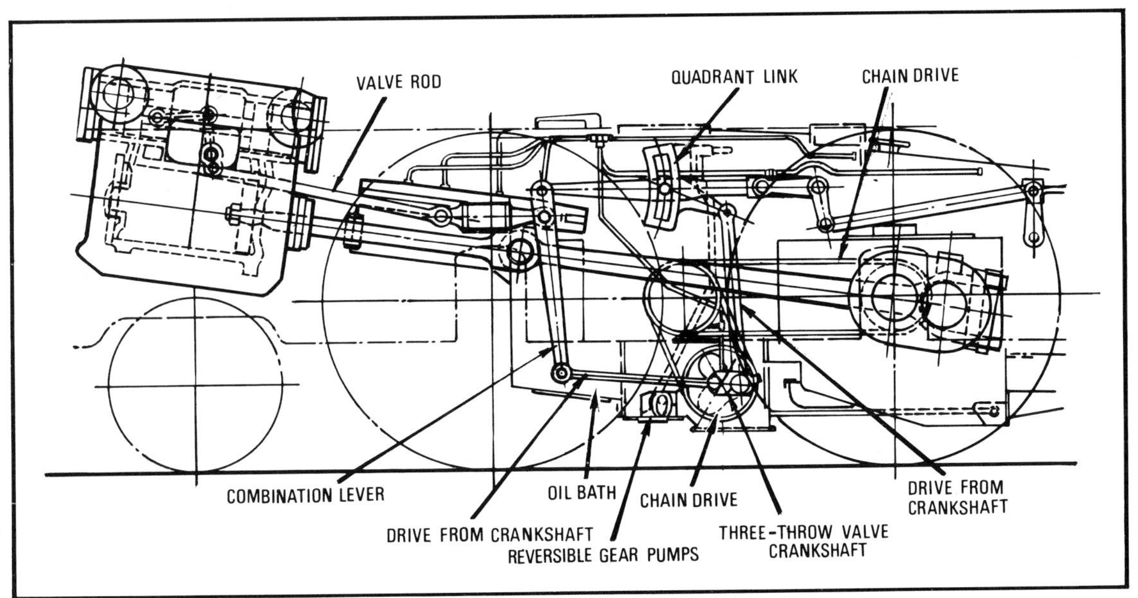

27
Bulleid's 'air-smoothed' exterior seen in 'Merchant Navy' 4-6-2 No 21C2 *Union Castle*. *BR*

28
One of the 'West Country' class light Pacifics, No 21C113 Okehampton. *BR*

which the base formed a sump for lubricating oil. There was no room between the frames for three sets of the orthodox connections from the crank axle to the expansion links and combination levers. These motions were therefore derived from a three-throw crankshaft separate from the crank axle and driven from it by chains (Fig 2). The chain drive was in two stages via an intermediate layshaft. Gear type pumps in the sump fed oil through distributor spray pipes to the moving parts. It was hoped that the oil would simply have to be topped up at works overhauls but in practice there was considerable leakage while running. The valve rods operated the valves through radial levers and it was found that this part of the gear rapidly got out of adjustment, while stretch in the chains caused further problems.

Undeterred, Bulleid retained these features in his

lighter 'West Country' Pacific series of 1945 but after nationalisation representatives of both classes were rebuilt with standard valve gear, losing their 'air smoothing' in the process. In this form both classes and the later 'Battle of Britain' Pacifics gave years of useful service.

When wartime traffic brought the need for more locomotives to do the work of Maunsell's 'Q' class, Bulleid did not add to their number but introduced his own 0-6-0, the 'Q1'. Keeping the same cylinder dimensions as in Class Q, he increased the boiler pressure, heating surface and grate area, basing his design on the 'Lord Nelson' firebox. The increased capacity had to be achieved within a weight of 54 tons, and with the boiler and firebox contributing an estimated 21¼ tons every possible means of saving weight elsewhere had to be exploited. The result was a 'basic locomotive' with no running plate or splashers, its coupled wheels fully exposed, and a starkly simple casing for the boiler. In appearance the 'Q1' stood in somewhat the same relation to the conventional locomotive as does the popular conception of Frankenstein's monster to the human species.

In the last years of the Southern Railway Bulleid was engaged on the design of his 'Leader' class locomotive. It ran on two six-wheel bogies, each with an integral steam engine, above which was what looked like a diesel locomotive body, with a cab at each end, but was in fact the casing of the boiler. The fireman's position was amidships. Trials of the sleeve valves developed for the 'Leader' took place on an ex-LBSC Atlantic before nationalisation but the first 'Leader' emerged in British Railways days. Its life was short, for after a few trial runs BR cancelled the order to build more locomotives of the same type and the pioneer 'Leader' was broken up, along with five sister engines which were never completed. Principal dimensions of steam locomotives built for the Southern Railway are shown in Table 2.

The Southern Railway announced that it was to build main line diesel-electric locomotives in 1947 but the first of them did not appear until 1951. Bulleid, in conjunction with the SR electrical engineer, Alfred Raworth, was also responsible for the first Southern Railway electric locomotive, which took the rails in 1942. This was a Co-Co for 660V dc with special provision for negotiating gaps in the conductor rail. Instead of the current energising the traction motors direct it did so via two motor-generator sets. Their output, opposing or 'boosting' the live rail voltage, was fed to the traction motors, and as each set had a flywheel on its shaft they continued revolving and generating current while none was being collected from the live rail because of a gap. With this arrangement the traction motor voltage could be controlled by small resistances in the generator field circuits, avoiding the losses incurred when resistances in the main power circuit are used for this purpose. All controller notches, and there were 26, could be used continuously. A second similar locomotive turned out in 1945 incorporated a few modifications introduced by C. M. Cock, who had succeeded Raworth as Electrical Engineer. The third and last of the class did not go into service until 1949, the second year of British Railways. By that time the Electrical Engineer of the Southern Region was S. B. Warder, later to become Chief Electrical Engineer of the British Transport Commission and the architect of the 25kV, 50Hz ac system of electrification on British Railways.

29
The first of Bulleid's 'Q1' class 'austerity' 0-6-0s. Note the 'alphanumeric' numbering, the letter 'C' standing for three coupled axles. *BR*

3 Rolling Stock

On its formation the Southern Railway took over 7,500 passenger vehicles. They were a varied assortment, including numbers of non-bogie coaches, and on the whole could be described as adequate by the standards of their day rather than distinguished. As late as 1933 the Southern had 84 four-wheeled and 405 six-wheeled coaches. The most recent pre-Grouping types were on the South Eastern & Chatham and the London & South Western. On the SE&CR a new Continental boat train had been introduced in 1921 and had been greeted by the comment in the railway press that 'this train is a departure from previous practice as up to now non-corridor stock has been used for boat trains on the South Eastern & Chatham Railway system'. These were bogie vehicles measuring 64ft over the gangways and were fitted with Pullman type couplers. A Pullman was included in the train for the service of refreshments. First class passengers could be served in their compartments, the coaches of this class having a cupboard for storing tables and crockery. The stock comprised first and second class coaches; first, second and third class brakes; first class brakes with a saloon section as well as compartments; and a brake composite with a similar layout. These coaches were used on Continental trains until the late 1930s and were later rebuilt in various ways for use on other services.

The London & South Western also introduced new main line corridor vehicles in 1921 to form four five-coach sets for Waterloo-Bournemouth trains. Each set consisted of a third class brake, a third class and a first class coach, a third class pantry vehicle, and another third class brake. The pantry was equipped with 'a boiler of a capacity sufficient to supply tea to all passengers', also an egg cooker and a grill. Portable tables could be fitted up in all compartments. The pantry facility was considered to be an alternative to 'the conventional tea basket', suitable for teas and light refreshments on services which did not call for full restaurant cars.

The Bournemouth stock, designed by S. Panter of the LSWR, measured 60ft 7in over buffers and had bogies with 7ft wheelbase at 41ft centres. The coaches were panelled externally with galvanised steel plates secured to a framing of oak and teak, from which they derived the nickname of 'Ironclads'. A five-coach set seated 42 first class and 184 third class passengers. Further 'Ironclads' were built by the Southern Railway and some lasted into British Railways days. As more vehicles came out of the works they were used to form the Weymouth portions of Bournemouth trains as well.

While Bournemouth had been relatively well looked after by the LSWR, passengers to the Kent coast resorts were still riding in non-corridor coaches. Maunsell turned his attention to these services and in 1924 introduced some eight-coach sets of corridor vehicles, each consisting of a third brake, a third class coach, four composites, a third class coach and a third brake. Overall length of each vehicle was 60ft. A Pullman car was included in the formation and refreshments could be served on tables fitted up in the compartments. The first working of the new stock was between Victoria and Ramsgate on 17 November 1924. It survived until the first phase of Kent Coast electrification in 1959.

The Kent Coast stock of 1924 was clearly SECR in parentage, and the same strain ran through more boat train stock in 1923/4. The matchboarded coach bodies were similar to the 1921 train but the body width was 8ft $6\frac{1}{2}$in. A new generation of specifically Southern rolling stock began with orders placed in 1925 for a series of corridor vehicles with a body length of 59ft and width 9ft to a standard design. The coaches were equipped with Pullman gangways and Buckeye couplers. On the non-corridor side there was a door to every compartment but the corridor side doors generally faced alternate compartments. Some of the stock formed three-coach sets for West of England services. Two eight-coach sets were allocated to the Central Section for Worthing and Eastbourne trains, and 11-coach sets were put on the Newhaven boat trains.

The 9ft body width was somewhat awkward on the Newhaven boat train because of restricted clearance in Lewes tunnel, and there were instructions that no other train was to pass through the tunnel at the same time. The tunnel had a sharp bend to the left at its southern end, the curvature of the down main line being of about 6ch radius. During the Eastbourne electrification works in the middle 1930s the tunnel was widened and the curvature eased to a minimum of 8ch. At the same time refuges were built in both tunnel walls at 90ft intervals.

While catering on the Central and Eastern Sections was provided from Pullman cars, the Western Section needed restaurant cars. The 1925 orders included six first class kitchen/restaurant cars and six third class restaurant cars (without kitchen). The first class car seated 24 in a two-and-one formation. One end of the car was occupied by a kitchen and a pantry separated by a passage 4ft 3in wide with sliding entry doors to each. The third class cars seated 64 passengers in pairs on each side of the gangway. Ten unclassed saloons built under the same orders differed from the other vehicles in being 8ft 6in wide.

More 8ft 6in vehicles were ordered in 1926, this time for Kent Coast and Eastbourne trains. Families going on holiday in those days brought much impedimenta with them and so the brake thirds had a large luggage space and only four compartments. In the following year four-coach sets of similar stock were ordered for the ex-SECR services from Charing Cross to Folkestone, Deal and Ramsgate, where previously three-coach non-corridor sets with lavatories had been the rule.

The Charing Cross-Hastings service then received attention. To meet the loading gauge restrictions on this route the bodies of the new vehicles were 58ft long and 8ft 0¾in wide. First class compartments seated three a side and third class four a side. It was pointed out that 'the reduced width of the stock tends to increase the comfort of the individual as the reduced number of seats allows more space for each person than that usually allotted'. Another feature extolled when the trains went into service in 1929 were the high window lights on the corridor side which enabled 'a very tall man to look out in comfort'. The Southern publicity department found a 'very tall man' and photographed him thus employed while smoking a pipe, an occupation not then held in disfavour. According to a press statement at the time the question of building new tunnels to overcome the loading gauge problems of the Hastings line had been considered, but the company concluded that 'the more economical way of benefiting passengers was by the construction of the special stock now being introduced'.

A new design of open third was included in the 1929 rolling stock orders. There were end entry vestibules with recessed doors and lavatories, and internally the saloon was divided into sections, one of four and one of three seating bays, with a total of 56 seats. These vehicles were intended mainly for use as third class restaurant cars, marshalled next to a first class restaurant/kitchen car. Another open coach described as a 'parlour saloon' was included in the programme. This was an 8ft 6in wide vehicle similar to the 'unclassed' series ordered in 1925. There were 42 seats, arranged two-and-one, in three sections with an entry door on each side. The partition doors between sections were hinged. Lavatories were provided in the end vestibules but there were no vestibule doors. Although this stock was not new in design, the Southern Railway chose an example for exhibition in a display of new rolling stock at Wimbledon in November 1931. The seats with 'fluted backs' and 'covered with tapestry' were evidently considered selling points.

A new series of unclassed saloon brakes of 8ft 6in body width was ordered in 1932, intended primarily for Continental boat trains. The 36 seats in the passenger section were divided between smoking and non-smoking areas, which were separated by a partition with a sliding door. Entry was by three doors on each side of the vehicle. A lavatory and a rack for luggage occupied part of a vestibule at the 'train' end of the coach. The seating pattern was two-and-one, and all seats had armrests. Between the doors there were large

30
Maunsell kitchen/buffet third No 7867. *LPC/IAL*

31
Maunsell 59ft corridor composite brake No 6686. *IAL*

fixed windows, each with a smaller sliding window above. Ten kitchen/dining cars ordered in the same programme were the last of Maunsell's design in this category to be built. One of them when new was exhibited at Wadebridge during celebrations of the Bodmin & Wadebridge Railway centenary in September 1934.

Orders in 1933 included open thirds with a new body styling. Windows were flush with the bodysides and the entry doors were recessed. The large windows had rectangular top corners but the lower corners were rounded, and each had two sliding ventilator glasses. Riveting of the external steel sheeting, with the rivet heads prominent, gave one observer the impression that 'the whole construction had been inspired by that of an armoured car'. This martial appearance was modified in the final phase of Maunsell's steam-hauled stock. The corridor coaches of 1935 had very large windows on the corridor side and the doors on this side were spaced so that they fell between compartments instead of opening directly on to them. It was hoped that this would avoid collision between passengers entering and those alighting. Windows were inserted from the inside and fixed panes had an external wooden moulding around them. A series of open thirds of the same design were fitted with 'Airstream' ventilators in the upper portion of fixed windows. Deflectors guided the incoming fresh air and the escaping used air so that air currents were kept at bay. The effect, to quote the official description, was that 'air in the vehicle is subject to continuous changes, and the rate of change can be regulated by moving the rear of the two movable frames in the direction of the train movement. Draughts are obviated'. There was clearly scope here for skilful manipulation but it is doubtful if the device was always used in the manner intended by the designer.

A characteristic Maunsell product was the General Utility Van, which stemmed from an earlier SECR vehicle. Its name summed up its usefulness for carrying practically any kind of article sent by passenger train, or for general freight service. The first Southern Railway version was a four-wheeled van with a body 32ft 4½in long, with double doors in the sides and at the ends. Building in various batches, some with a 32ft 6¾in body, extended from 1925 to 1937. Another version had a less comprehensive title, being simply designated 'luggage vans', and had side doors only. They came into service in 1935.

In 1930 the building of bogie luggage vans began, using underframes released when the bodies of ex-LSWR suburban coaches were mounted on new underframes to form electric sets. Body lengths of the vans were 51ft 3in and 53ft 3in, with three double doors in each side. The ex-LSW underframes were lengthened as necessary. These vans were mainly used on the Western Section. A batch authorised in 1936 was built with a central guard's compartment and the same arrangement was adopted in a later series of vehicles.

Three special four-wheeled vans were built for the through London/Paris 'Night Ferry' service of 1936. They had dual (vacuum and Westinghouse) braking, steam heat and electric lighting. A central roof lookout was provided to meet French requirements. The vans were painted blue, with yellow lettering, matching the livery of the Wagons-Lits stock in the rest of the train.

32
After ending its days as a staff van, DS70034, a Maunsell brake stands in dilapidated condition at Swindon in 1979. *C. Burnham*

33
Two of Maunsell's general utility vans in company with an ex-LCDR bogie brake, which had survived into the 1950s. *IAL*

34
Third class compartment of Bulleid postwar mainline stock. *BR*

35
Pantry unit in one of Bulleid's restaurant-kitchen cars for the six-coach Bournemouth sets of 1947. *BR*

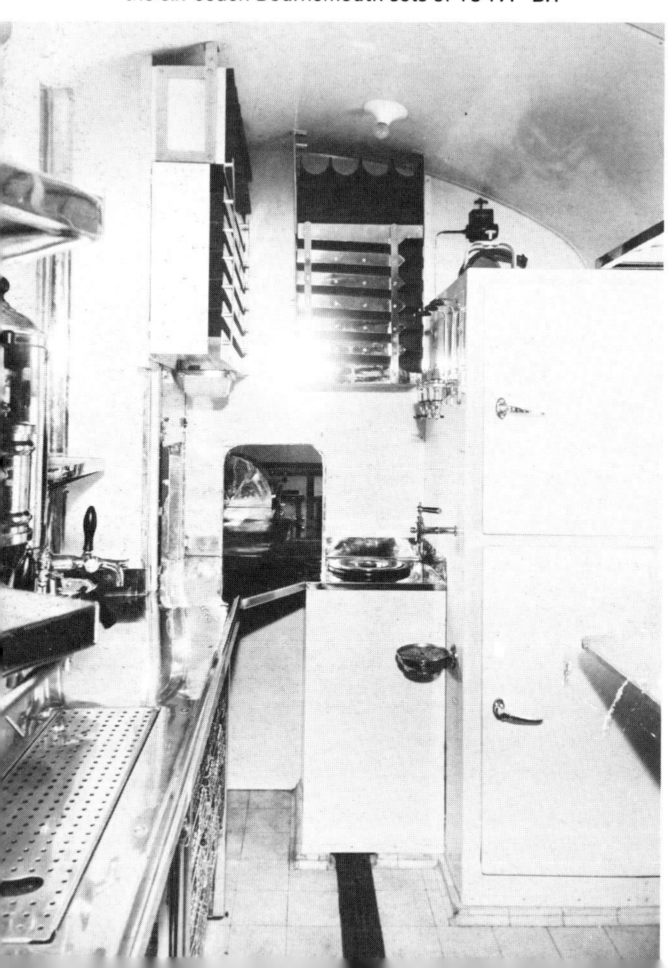

Lugs on the solebars enabled them to be secured by chains during the ferry crossing. Dimensions were 36ft over headstocks and a wheelbase of 23ft. Similar dimensions were used in a standard four-wheeled guard's van introduced in 1937, having a central guard's compartment flanked by two luggage compartments, each with two double doors.

Maunsell retired on 31 October 1937 and was succeeded by O. V. S. Bulleid. The first distinctive new vehicles of the Bulleid era were his buffet cars for the Mid-Sussex electrification of 1938. In the same year Bulleid refurbished two 11-coach trains for the 'Bournemouth Limited' service, painting them externally in malachite green. Eventually three more sets and seven 'Schools' 4-4-0 locomotives were treated similarly for working the same train. The idea of streamlining a 'Schools' had been toyed with but dropped after a short experiment. Clearly the public was impressed by the streamlined trains on the northern lines and the Southern, increasingly indentified with efficient but hardly charismatic main line emus, wanted a share of the admiration. In the end it settled for an updated image by other means.

The compartment walls and ceilings in the refurbished 'Bournemouth Limited' stock were covered with Rexine, pale yellow in the firsts and stone colour in the thirds. Upholstery was pale green and pale pink respectively. Seats in all compartments had individual backs. Other changes were tubular lamps and more heating in the firsts, and framed paintings replacing maps and advertisements in the thirds. The first class kitchen/dining cars in these trains were refurnished with individual seats, green Wilton carpet, and original water-colours on the walls. Ventilation was improved by roof-mounted extractor fans. Two thirds and two composites not normally included in the train sets were treated similarly so that if the train needed strengthening it would present the same image from locomotive to rear brake.

The Railway Gazette of 29 July 1938 said of the trains: 'Externally they are painted a plain unlined bright green; and headed by one of the handsome and efficient "Schools" class engines similarly coloured but with conventional black and white lining present a very striking appearance . . . Truly Mr Bulleid is to be congratulated on his first effort in cheering the passenger by congenial surroundings'.

Bulleid's first new coaches for steam-hauled trains were put in hand just before World War 2; work began on the underframes but was then suspended and the stock was not completed until 1945/6. It comprised three-coach sets consisting of two third class brakes and a composite, all retaining Maunsell's 59ft body length. The Bulleid hallmarks in vehicles otherwise generally similar to their predecessors were the lozenge-shaped toplights above the droplights in the doors and the continuous curve of the bodysides, matched by curved glass in the windows, giving more width in the compartments at shoulder level.

The Southern now revealed its thinking on passenger stock for the postwar years by exhibiting a prototype corridor composite. Four first class and three third class compartments were provided in a body 64ft 6in long as compared with Maunsell's standard 59ft. The public was invited to comment on the appointments and their views were taken into account in future designs, although a strong preference for compartments was not always fully reflected in the proportion of compartment to saloon seating. The first production vehicles with the new body length were 24 three-coach sets consisting of two brake thirds and a composite having the same layout as the prototype. They began going into service in December 1946 on the 'Atlantic Coast Express'.

Next to be built were 11 six-coach sets for the Waterloo-Bournemouth service, each consisting of a third brake, a composite, a restaurant first, restaurant/kitchen car, an open third and a third brake. The restaurant first provided 24 seats for diners and three first class compartments (later fitted with tables to increase the number who could be served). The adjacent restaurant/kitchen car had a third class saloon with 32 seats. Layout of the composite was similar to the prototype, the two blocks of compartments being separated by a transverse vestibule. The three entry doors on each side of the coach gave access respectively to this centre vestibule and to the vestibules at the ends. There was a similar pattern of doors and vestibules in the open third. The first set went into service in September 1947.

One of the features of the prototype put into practice in this stock were the electrically-heated foot mats between the compartment seats. The maximum heat was slightly below blood heat but its effect was said to be appreciable. Power for the mats was taken from 230V axle-driven generators but other heating was by steam. Contemporary comment approved the hammock-sprung seats, although *The Railway Gazette* returned to one of its recurrent themes of those days and criticised the shape of the seat backs.

The Southern Railway's Royal Train was the train which had served the South Eastern & Chatham. It included a Royal Saloon which had been built by the South Eastern Railway in 1903. With a body only 8ft 1in wide, this vehicle could travel on the Tunbridge Wells-Hastings line if necessary. The length was 50ft, and the saloon was carried on bogies with 8ft wheelbase. Internally there were two compartments furnished in different styles, one of them the King's and the other the Queen's. Other coaches in the train were two corridor saloons, a non-gangwayed saloon, a side corridor coach, and two saloon brakes. When the Southern took the train over it was painted green with white roofs.

To ease the load on its works imposed by postwar reconstruction the Southern went to outside industry for some of its requirements. In 1947 it received the first of 35 three-coach sets being built by the Birmingham Railway Carriage & Wagon Co Ltd. The third class brakes in these sets had the unusual arrangement of a four-seat coupé compartment. The remaining accommodation in these vehicles was an eight-seat ordinary compartment separated by a transverse entry vestibule from a saloon with four seating bays. The compartments in this stock were similar to those of the prototype coach.

Statistics of freight rolling stock come as a surprise considering that the Southern was primarily a passenger line. In 1934 the company possessed 24,469 open wagons, of which 24,375 were of a capacity of between 8 and 12 tons; 5,054 covered wagons, practically all of between 8 and 12 tons capacity; 851 mineral wagons, 2,770 wagons for special traffic, for

36
A six-a-side compartment in Bulleid's postwar four-car electric suburban stock. *John Topham*

cattle and for rails and timber, and 928 goods brakes. Some of the brake vans were bogie vehicles built on the underframes of the motor luggage vans of the ac electrification to Sutton and Coulsdon. When more carriage underframes became available because the bodywork was used in new dc electric stock, Maunsell used 90 of them to build bogie passenger luggage vans of 10 tons capacity. Body lengths were 50ft 11in and 48ft 11in, and the width 8ft 0½in. The roof design enabled these vehicles to travel on the Tonbridge-Hastings line.

An unusual design of vehicle was a four-wheel wagon for milk traffic between Cole, Somerset, and Clapham Junction. It was arranged to carry road trailer milk tanks of 2,000gal capacity which were hauled up a hinged ramp on to runways on the wagon underframe by a motor tractor at the loading point. Pulleys to guide the wire haulage rope were pivoted at both ends of the wagon and the equipment included wheel chocks. The load was 15 tons, and the wagons

37/38
A contrast in Southern Railway goods brakes — a four-wheel vehicle and one of the eight-wheelers using the underframe of former ac motor-luggage vans employed on the Sutton/Coulsdon electrification.
LPC/IAL and C. Burnham

39
A 10-ton open wagon. *LPC/IAL*

could run in passenger trains, being vacuum-braked, with steam heating pipes.

In 1927 the Southern received from Charles Roberts & Co Ltd two bogie freight wagons for exceptional loads. The well floor, consisting of moveable crossbars, could take a distributed load of 30 tons. Tare weight was approximately 22ton 12cwt, and length over buffers 58ft. A load of 20 tons could be carried over each bogie. Wheel diameter was 2ft 9in and the bogie wheelbase 5ft 6in.

40
United Dairies began milk transport by rail in glass-lined tank wagons in 1927. The vehicle illustrated was built in 1931. *BR*

41
Ballast from Meldon Quarries for relaying all over the system was conveyed in 40-ton steel hopper wagons. *IAL*

4 Engineering

NEW LINES

Torrington to Halwill Junction

The LSWR line through Barnstaple turned south to terminate at Torrington, some 20 miles from Halwill Junction where the lines to Bude and Padstow diverged. Construction of a railway between Halwill and Torrington was authorised in 1914, powers being given to a North Cornwall & Devon Railway Company. Work was delayed by the war and did not begin until 30 June 1922. The line was not opened until 27 July 1925, by which time the Southern Railway was in being and took over on a lease. There were seven intermediate stations or halts. From Halwill Junction, 600ft above sea level, to Torrington, at an altitude of 77ft, the generally falling tendency of the route was broken by some sharp undulations. Between Hatherleigh and Meeth Halt a ridge was crossed with a climb of 1 in 38/42, followed by a similar descent. In the final stages of the journey there was a short but sharp 1 in 50 to contend with before the line descended to the valley in which Torrington is situated.

Clay and lignite workings at Meeth were the principal sources of traffic. Passenger traffic was satisfactory in the early years but never heavy in spite of the hopes of the promoters, who pointed to substantial savings in rail distances via the new line and saw Halwill becoming 'one of the largest and most important junctions on a single line in the United Kingdom'.

Wimbledon & Sutton Railway

In 1924 the Southern Railway took over the powers of the Wimbledon & Sutton Railway, which had been authorised in 1910 and was to have been worked by the Metropolitan District Railway. The project was not put in hand, however, but it was revived in 1923 when the Southern Railway saw a proposed extension of the City & South London tube into the area as an unjustified intrusion into its suburban territory. It was then agreed that the City & South London should not extend beyond Morden and that the Southern should build the Wimbledon & Sutton line. Construction began at the Wimbledon end in 1927 and the line was opened to South Merton on 6 July 1929, and to a junction with the Central Section at Sutton on 5 January 1930. Six new stations were built, all with island platforms. At St Helier, where the LCC was establishing an estate of about 10,000 houses, there was a sizeable goods yard but elsewhere only passenger train traffic was dealt with. The line cost about £1million to build as it required much high embankment to carry it over roads, and had a total of 24 bridges, one of them with a span of 120ft.

The line was electrified from the outset. With gradients as steep as 1 in 49 and 1 in 44 approaching Sutton, and other sections at 1 in 60, working with steam would have been difficult. Signalling was with upper-quadrant semaphores. In the original Wimbledon & Sutton Railway plans the junction at Wimbledon would have been with the tracks used by District trains on the north side of the station, but as built the line entered the south side of the station and joined the former LBSC & LSW Joint tracks to Haydons Road and Streatham Junction. Train services over the line ran between Holborn Viaduct and West Croydon.

Allhallows branch

With considerable optimism a development company in the 1930s sought to establish a new seaside resort and coastal suburb for Londoners at Allhallows on the North Kent coast, looking across the Thames Estuary towards Southend-on-Sea. Publicity material described Allhallows-on-Sea as being 'laid out in the most approved and up-to-date manner with tree-lined avenues and a concrete approach road, whilst it also boasts a fine stretch of firm sand'. The Southern's Gravesend-Port Victoria line passed close to the site and a single-track branch, 1¾mile long, was built to serve it from near Middle Stoke Halt. The branch was opened on 16 May 1932 (special excursions had been run over it on 14 May). A second track was added in 1965. Services were mainly to and from Gravesend but there were a few London through trains. The branch was never electrified for when electrification was extended eastward from Gravesend in 1939 the Port Victoria line was not included in the scheme.

Motspur Park to Chessington

Rapid housing development in the area around Chessington, Surrey, in the mid-1930s led to the decision to tap the potential commuter traffic by building a branch from the Raynes Park-Epsom line at Motspur Park. The branch was $4\frac{1}{4}$ miles long and traversed undulating country with a heavy clay subsoil. Most of the route was on embankment or in cuttings, necessitating special measures because of the nature of the ground. Embankments were stabilised with dry filling material from slum clearance and other demolition work in London. At the terminus, Chessington South, the station platform (an island) and goods yard were in cutting with the unusual feature that 6in of concrete was laid as a 'floor' under 8in ballast. The clay excavated was run back in tip-up trucks over the contractor's narrow-gauge line to Tolworth, where a heavy fill was required, the station being on a 20ft bank. Tolworth goods yard, adjacent to the station, could accommodate 218 wagons in seven sidings and was provided with cart roads, a goods shed, and offices.

A dip to the point where the line crossed the Hogsmill river on a bridge 140ft long was at 1 in 98 on both sides. This was followed by a climb at 1 in 100 and 1 in 159 to the bridge crossing the Ewell-Epsom road at Tolworth. There was then a further drop at 1 in 100 before the line rose steadily to Chessington South, again with 1 in 100 as the steepest gradient. At Chessington South the goods yard was beyond the station. It had been proposed to continue the line to Leatherhead but this never materialised.

The branch was opened to Tolworth on 29 May 1938 and extended to Chessington South on 28 May 1939. Chessington South is the station for Chessington Zoo and at the opening ceremony the Deputy Mayor of Surbiton was photographed exchanging greetings with a baby elephant from that establishment.

There were 11 bridges on the line, all of steel girders encased in concrete. Fencing throughout was of a new diamond mesh pattern between concrete posts which had been adopted by the Southern for its electrified lines to prevent trespass.

At Malden Manor and Tolworth the platforms were roofed for 200ft with Chisarc cantilevered reinfored concrete roofing, requiring no supports. Lighting under the roofs was by cold cathode fluorescent tubes, while by day the appearance was lightened by small circular glass lenses let into the concrete. All stations were planned with forecourts providing space for car parking. When the first section to Tolworth was opened the Southern's Traffic Manager, Eustace

42
Malden Manor station on the Chessington branch, showing the special form of platform awning characteristic of this section of the Southern Electric system. *BR*

J. Missenden, quoted figures showing how fast the company's commuter traffic was developing. A recent census at Southern termini in London had shown that 733,500 passengers used these stations on a normal day, an increase of nearly 42% over 10 years previously. He contrasted the density of traffic on the Southern Railway with the situation in the United States where a railway system of nearly 242,000 route-miles had carried 490million passengers in 1936. On the Southern Railway, with a route-mileage of 2,200, the number carried in 1937 had been 378million.

Totton to Fawley

A company had been formed before World War 1 to build a railway to serve Hythe and Fawley on the west bank of Southampton Water, an area to which the only public transport had been by ferry between Southampton and Hythe. No action was taken until after the war, the Totton, Hythe & Fawley Light Railway Company being merged with the Southern Railway, which built the line. It was single track throughout, with intermediate stations at Marchwood and Hythe, and in a total length of some nine miles had no gradient steeper than 1 in 200. The branch left the main line to Bournemouth at Eling signalbox, immediately west of Totton station. It was operated as one block section, the train staff being picked up and dropped at Eling box. There were sidings for local factories at Hythe, and at Fawley a siding led through a gate to the Agwy petroleum works and Calshott aerodrome. Traffic began on 20 July 1925. Most trains were through to and from Southampton Docks (later Southampton Terminus). Today the branch is freight only, serving the huge Esso refinery at Fawley and Marchwood power station. Agwy Petroleum is a forgotten name.

Ramsgate-Margate link

The SECR inherited separate stations at Ramsgate from its South Eastern and London Chatham & Dover constituents, both of them terminals. They were by-passed by a new line about $1\frac{1}{2}$ miles long opened on 2 July 1926 between St Lawrence on the South Eastern line and a point south of Broadstairs on the LCDR. A new Ramsgate station was built on this line; also a station at Dumpton Park. The previous Ramsgate stations were closed. Trains for Margate from the Ashford direction had previously had to reverse in the SER Ramsgate Town station, continuing to Margate Sands. Under the new arrangement the SER Ramsgate-Margate line and Margate Sands station were closed and trains by the South Eastern route joined the LCDR line via Broadstairs by means of the new connection, running into the former LCDR Margate West station, now renamed Margate (Fig 3).

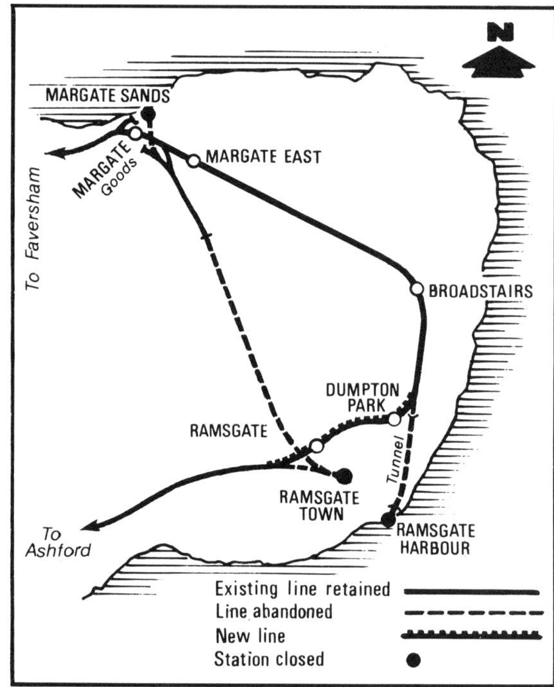

Fig 3
Station alterations in the Margate/Ramsgate area

Curves at Lewisham

Improvements in connections between the LCDR and SER systems had been begun by the South Eastern & Chatham Joint Committee. The Southern Railway continued the process by building two short curves at Lewisham, opened on 7 July 1929 (Fig 4). One of these was of major importance for freight traffic, since it provided a new route to Hither Green marshalling yard for trains from the LMSR (Midland Division) and LNER (GN Section) travelling to the Southern via the Metropolitan Widened Lines. About a mile of the Greenwich Park branch east of Brockley Lane was rehabilitated (since closure of the branch in 1917 the Nunhead-Brockley Lane section had only carried traffic to two coal depots) and was connected with a new curve to the ex-SER main line to Hither Green. Freight which previously had joined the SER line by the spur from Blackfriars Junction to Metropolitan Junction could now avoid the congested area through London Bridge, travelling via Loughborough Junction, Nunhead and the new curve. Traffic from the LMS (Western Division) and the Great Western via the West London Extension line was also given direct access to Hither Green by this connection.

The second curve at Lewisham put Lewisham

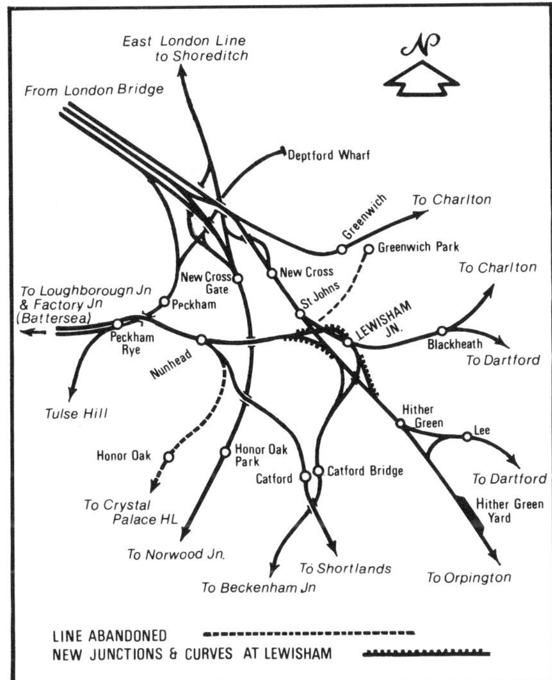

Fig 4
New curves at Lewisham providing improved connections to Hither Green yard for cross-London traffic

station (then Lewisham Junction) on a loop off the main line between St Johns and Hither Green, enabling more suburban services to be routed through this busy centre.

Flying and burrowing junctions

The flyover at Wimbledon opened in 1936 brought the number of flying and burrowing junctions on the Southern Railway up to 25, of which 22 were in the suburban and inner suburban areas. The Wimbledon flyover was of steel and concrete construction; a bridge of nine spans was approached in the up direction by a gradient of 1 in 60, followed by a drop of 1 in 45 as the up local line descended to the same level as the down local. It was now possible for a train approaching Waterloo on the up local to enter its platform at Waterloo without crossing other lines en route.

There was a long tradition of flyovers on constituents of the Southern Railway, dating back to the London & Croydon Railway's atmospheric venture in 1845 when the atmospheric line crossed over the ordinary line in this manner near Norwood. A full account of all the Southern Railway's flying and burrowing junctions was given in *The Railway Gazette* of 6 and 13 November 1936 (see bibliography). A

43
Flyover at St Johns (Lewisham). *Alan A. Jackson*

44
The up local line crosses the through lines on the Wimbledon flyover, descending to continue to Waterloo next to the down local line seen on the right with an electric train on the Kingston 'roundabout' service. Durnsford Road power station is in the background. *BR*

45
Main line electrification in the 1930s was accompanied by widespread rebuilding of stations. Work is in progress here at Horsham on the former LBSC route to Bognor and Portsmouth via the Mid-Sussex line. *BR*

46
During diversions for tunnel repairs, a Charing Cross-Ashford train takes the loop from Chiselhurst to join the ex-LCDR line at St Mary Cray. The locomotive is 'King Arthur' No 806 *Sir Galleron*. *R. W. Beaton*

47
Calstock Viaduct on the branch from Bere Alston, with the hoist for lifting wagons from the quay on the River Tamar. *H. C. Casserley*

48
Meldon Viaduct, near Okehampton, with a 'West Country' Pacific heading the Cornwall portion of the up 'Atlantic Coast Express' *John Parsons*

simple arrangement which developed into one of considerable complexity was seen at Norwood Junction. It began when the LBSC opened an additional down line which bridged over the up and down main lines to join the West Croydon branch. From this beginning in 1857 there grew the elaborate system of interconnections shown in Fig 5. It is put on record here because track rationalisation in progress on the Central Section of the Southern Region at the time of writing is likely to efface its memory.

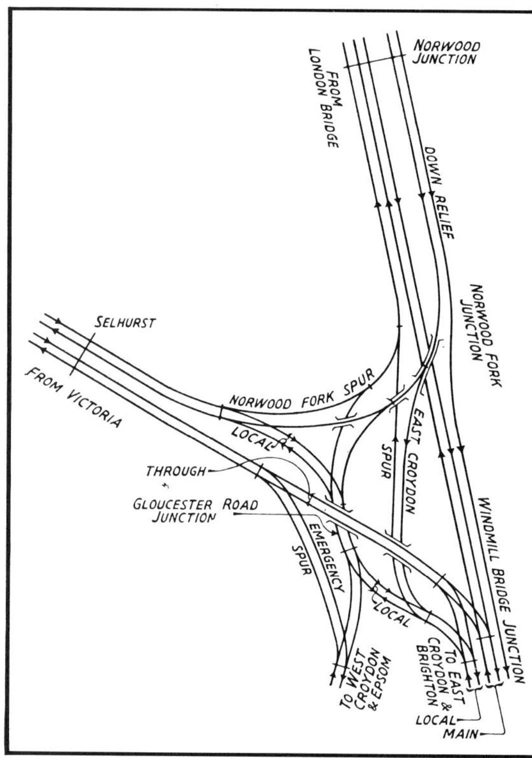

Fig 5
The Norwood Junction complex. (By courtesy of *The Railway Gazette*).

SIGNALLING

Predecessors of the Southern Railway made noteworthy contributions to signalling development. Some of their work remained in service throughout the Grouping years and beyond. The gantries of automatic lower-quadrant semaphores spanning the four-track main line of the Western Section between Woking and Basingstoke, a stop and a distant arm on each post, lasted until electrification of the Bournemouth main line in 1967. This was a low-pressure electro-pneumatic system with an air supply at 25lb/sq in. Air was fed to diaphragm valves which operated the signal arms under the control of the track circuits. With a track circuit unoccupied, the track relay was energised and current passed through its contact to a magnet valve. Air was admitted to operate a piston and lower the stop signal arm.

Contacts on the signal arm controlled two functions. If the stop signal ahead was 'off', one of the contacts completed a circuit to lower the distant arm; the second contact acted similarly for the distant in rear.

When a train entered the track circuit the track relay dropped and broke the circuit to the magnet valve controlling the stop arm, which went to 'danger'. In doing so, the arm broke the circuits to the distant arms, setting both at 'Caution'.

After the train had cleared the track circuit the stop arm was lowered as before, but the distant did not clear until the stop arm of the signal ahead was 'off'.

Signalling development on the Southern Railway was closely linked with the spread of electrification, and the new traffic conditions created by the electric trains were responsible for the large installations of colour-lights and power boxes undertaken by the company in the busiest areas. W. J. Thorowgood, the Signal & Telegraph Superintendent, was a member of the Three-Position Signal Committee set up by the Institution of Railway Signal Engineers in 1924 to establish a code of practice on aspects. He was faced with the imminent arrival of electric trains on the crowded approaches to the London termini of the former South Eastern & Chatham Railway, and it was agreed by the Committee that, to meet the situation of steam and electric trains with very different acceleration and braking characteristics sharing the same tracks, a fourth signal aspect would be necessary. The members were also in agreement that the colour-light would be the signal of the future on the railways of Great Britain. Therefore the new work on the South Eastern lines in the London area was all planned on the basis of colour-light signals with three and four aspects.

49
Stop and distant arms of the electro-pneumatic semaphores at Woking are 'off' for a train to the West Country headed by 'Scotch Arthur' No 780 *Sir Persant. Geoffrey J. Jefferson*

50
Miniature levers operating signals and points in the power box at Woking which replaced three manual boxes. *BR*

SOUTHERN
780

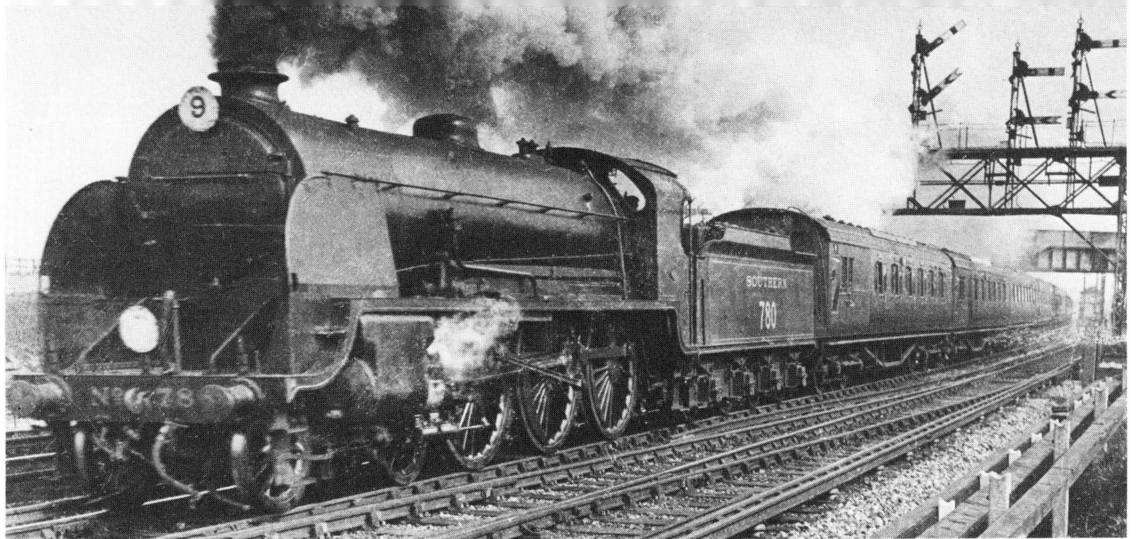

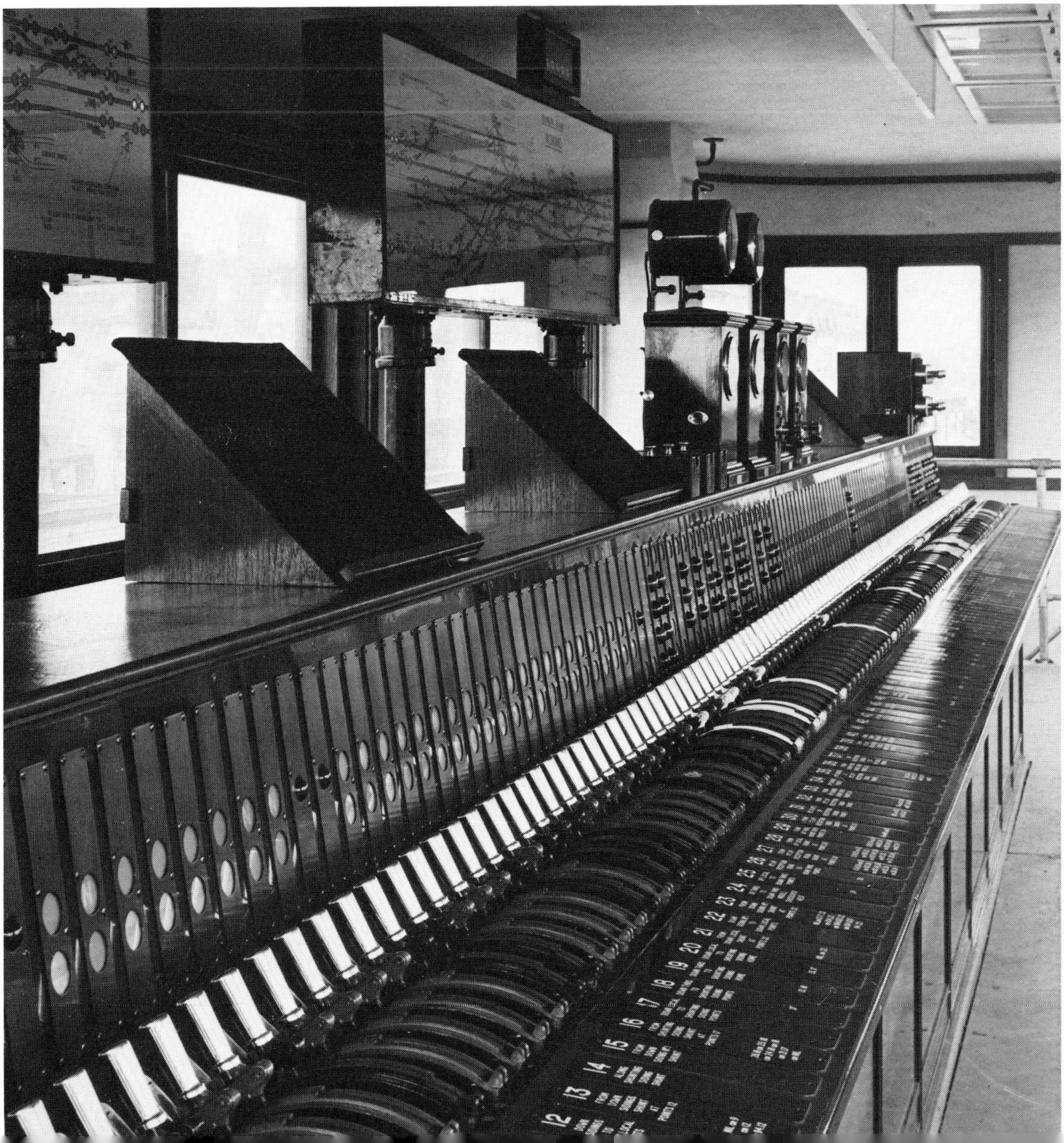
12
13
14
15
16
17
18
19
20
21
22
23
24

51
The manual signalbox at Guildford. Colour-lights replaced semaphores as a preliminary to the 'Direct Portsmouth' electrification. *BR*

52
The eve of the changeover to colour-lights between Elephant & Castle and Holborn Viaduct in March 1926, with the new signals and the old semaphores side by side. *BR*

The first application of four-aspect colour-light signalling was on the line between Elephant & Castle, St Pauls and Holborn Viaduct, where it was brought into use on 21 March 1926. Boxes at Holborn Viaduct and Blackfriars Junction controlled the area, displacing seven previous mechanical boxes. At Holborn Viaduct the old box was retained but a power frame was installed and a relay room added. An entirely new building was provided at Blackfriars Junction. The levers in the power frames were $4\frac{1}{2}$in long, with a stroke of $5\frac{1}{2}$in. At Blackfriars Junction there were 120 levers in a frame 258ft long. Holborn Viaduct controlled as far as St Pauls (now Blackfriars), while Blackfriars Junction controlled from there to Elephant & Castle together with part of the spur to Metropolitan Junction on the South Eastern line.

Electric point machines were installed throughout the area and there were 112 multi-aspect colour-light signals. Where short sighting distances made repeaters necessary these took the form of auxiliary signals which could show green, single yellow or double yellow. They had no red aspect, but a white cross on a black ground was illuminated when the main signal was showing red. This arrangement overcame the drawback of a driver having to pass a red aspect shown by a repeater.

At this period the power frame levers were locked electrically against false operation, but the interlocking between levers was mechanical. The same principle was followed in the new frames for the resignalling out of Charing Cross which also began in 1926. Charing Cross, Metropolitan Junction and Cannon Street were resignalled in June of that year. In June 1928 Borough Market Junction and London Bridge were dealt with.

Installing the 311-lever frame at London Bridge was a delicate task because of the precise levelling and alignment necessary to ensure smooth operation of the interlocking, some of the bars being very long in order to act on widely separated levers. Although the Cannon Street frame, with 143 levers, was shorter, the interlocking was exceptionally complex and when modifications were required the inconvenience of the mechanical system was only too apparent.

In the meantime all-electric interlocking had been developed. It was first installed on the Southern Railway at North Kent East Junction, between London Bridge and New Cross, where resignalling

53
Four-aspect signals with route indicators and shunt signals at Cannon Street, resignalled in June 1926. *IAL*

54
While the new Waterloo and Victoria boxes were even more box-like than the traditional signalbox, a new style was emerging and is exemplified by the building at Surbiton for the Waterloo-Hampton Court Junction resignalling. *BR*

was commissioned in December 1929. All subsequent Southern Railway power frames were interlocked electrically.

Colour-light signalling did not come to Waterloo until 1936. This was the final step in a colour-light scheme extending from Hampton Court Junction to the terminus. One phase of the work was the Wimbledon flyover which rearranged the order of tracks inward from that point, carrying the up main local line across the up and down main through lines. On the 'country' side of the flyover the up and down through lines were between the local lines. From the flyover to Waterloo the arrangement (north to south) became up through, down through, up local, down local (Fig 6).

The new all-electric box at Waterloo was opened on

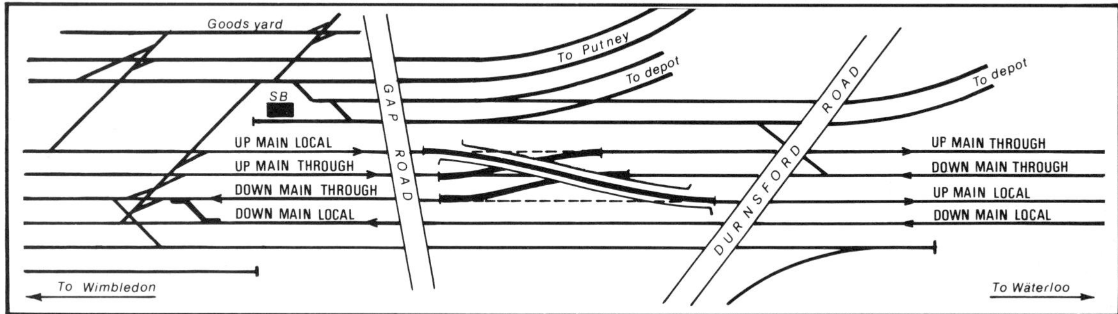

Fig 6
Diagram showing rearrangement of tracks north of Wimbledon by the flyover at Durnsford Road (New connections bold; connections removed dotted). (By courtesy of *The Railway Magazine*).

Table 3 — Waterloo-Hampton Court Junction resignalling

Old arrangement

Box	*No of levers*
Waterloo 'A'	262
Waterloo 'B'	100
Waterloo 'C'	35
Vauxhall 'D'	23
Vauxhall East	29
Vauxhall West	50
Loco Junction	92
Queens Road East	48
Queens Road West	64
West London Junction	52
Clapham Junction 'A'	108
Clapham Junction 'D'	16
Clapham Cutting	15
Earlsfield	28
Durnsford Road	41
Wimbledon 'A'	130
Wimbledon 'B'	64
Wimbledon 'C'	60
Raynes Park	48
Malden	47
Marsh Lane	18
Surbiton	63
Hampton Court Junction	60

Revised (1936) arrangement

Box	*No of levers*
Waterloo (New)	309
Loco Junction	92
Queens Road	64
West London Junction	59
Clapham Junction 'A'	103
Earlsfield	28
Wimbledon 'A'	130
Wimbledon 'B'	64
Wimbledon 'C'	60
Raynes Park	48
Malden	47
Surbiton (New)	52
Hampton Court Junction (New)	45

18 October 1936, replacing the 'A' box which had been in service for some 44 years. There were three frames, with 75, 159 and 75 levers, and the new box replaced six mechanical boxes with a total of 499 levers. Points were worked by 134 point machines powered from a battery charged by metal rectifiers. The old and new signalling arrangements between Waterloo and Hampton Court Junction are compared in Table 3.

In 1939 Woking was the only complete power scheme, with electric locking, outside the London area. Elsewhere upper-quadrant semaphores were general, with distants worked by electric signal machines. Electric point machines were used for points too far from a box to be worked manually.

As colour-lights replaced semaphores the use of splitting signals at junctions became obsolete and junction indications were given by inclined rows of three white lights (illuminated only when a diverging route was set). The principle was similar to the five-light indicator standardised by British Railways in later years. Multi-lamp route indicators showing a letter or figure were used at termini. Where semaphore signalling was in use mechanical indicators showed a black figure or letter on a white background. When the signal was 'on' a black disc was displayed. When the signal was pulled 'off' the disc fell away and the appropriate symbol came into view. The largest indicator of this type at Waterloo before the resignalling could show 16 routes.

Considerable use was made of intermediate signalling with two-aspect colour-lights on steeply graded lines where ascending trains took much longer to clear a block section than those running downhill. Provided the intermediate signal was 'on', a signalman could clear his starting signal for a train to proceed although

55
One of the three miniature lever frames in the power signalbox at Waterloo, commissioned in 1936. *IAL*

56
Waterloo power box in BR days. *BR*

57
Two-aspect intermediate colour-light mounted on apparatus case. *IAL*

he had not yet received a release from the box ahead. The intermediate signal was in effect an intermediate unattended block post and was preceded by a distant signal, but it was actually an advanced starter. This type of signalling was first installed on the up line between Winchester and Worting Junction where there was an up grade of about 1 in 252 for 16 miles. One of the most useful applications was on Sole Street bank on the Eastern Section where the up line gradient was 1 in 100 for five miles and at times of heavy holiday traffic there were often long delays because of the time trains took to clear the block sections. These intermediate signals were mounted on a tubular post on top of the apparatus case containing the controlling relays.

The last of the Southern's London termini to be resignalled was Victoria. On the Central Section the work between Pouparts Junction and station limits was commissioned on 16 October 1938, an all-electric frame being installed at Battersea Park Junction. At Victoria the Central Section box had been equipped with the W. R. Sykes electro-mechanical system in 1908, with miniature slides above the point levers for working the signals. Shortly before Grouping, however, the slide mechanism was removed and a relay system installed. On 3/4 June 1939 a new power box with a 225-lever all-electric frame took over the whole of the working on the Central Section side of the station. The installation comprised 90 pairs of points and 145 signals.

The Eastern Section side of the station had been resignalled by the SECR in 1919 with electrically-worked upper-quadrant three-position semaphores. Much of the equipment could be adapted to current Southern Railway practice and the two existing signal-boxes were retained but the power frame locking was

58
The power frame in the Victoria (Eastern) signalbox modernised with new panel indications and lever nameplates for the 1939 resignalling. *IAL*

59
The new Central Section box at Victoria in 1939. *IAL*

revised. The work was carried out in stages, including replacement of the electrically-worked semaphores, and was completed on 25 June 1939.

WORKS AND MOTIVE POWER DEPOTS

The Southern Railway made Eastleigh its main works for locomotive and carriage construction. Carriage and wagon building for the LSWR had been transferred to Eastleigh from Nine Elms in 1890, the Locomotive Department following in 1909. At Grouping the locomotive side was reorganised to achieve a quicker throughput of engines under repair, and more room was made available for building steam and electric stock by transferring carriage repairs to the ex-LBSC works at Lancing. This works also built goods brakes and Maunsell's 'general utility' vans, and installed the Westinghouse brake and traction equipment in emus. Lancing itself had been an 'overflow' works, coming into full operation in 1912 to relieve pressure on the works at Brighton where extension was impracticable.

Brighton works continued building locomotives until 1929, after which most of its activities were transferred to Eastleigh and the former South Eastern Railway works at Ashford. In World War 2, however, Brighton was re-equipped for war work and was again building locomotives in the postwar years. Wagon building for the Southern Railway was concentrated at Ashford, which had turned out its first locomotives in 1853. A chemical laboratory established by the SECR in 1915 was extended by the Southern Railway.

There were several improvements to locomotive depots in Southern Railway days. At Dover the town had been served by the Priory station since the building of Dover Marine for Continental traffic and closure of the former Town and Pier stations. The Southern announced improvements at Dover Priory in 1925 which involved moving the locomotive depot to a new site. Previously it had occupied a considerable portion of the space available between the Priory and Harbour tunnels. The new site was at Archcliffe Fort, then being demolished and adjacent to the site of the old Town station. Here accommodation was provided for about 30 locomotives. Clearance of the ground at Priory allowed a large goods shed to be built with accommodation for about 114 wagons; the old shed could only take about 50. At the same time passenger facilities were improved by lengthening the platforms to 700ft. Previously the down platform had been 500ft and the up only 200ft in length and maximum width had been 12ft. The new platforms were 22ft wide.

Improvements were also carried out at Exmouth Junction, Feltham, Ashford, Norwood and Stewarts Lane, and a new depot was built at Hither Green. Modernisation at Stewarts Lane was accompanied by closure of the LBSCR Battersea depot and transfer of its locomotives to the new shed. This depot was at the point where the original low-level LBSC and LCDR approach lines to Victoria converged. It was now provided with a mechanical coaling plant having a capacity of 150,000ton/hr and a water softening plant which could treat 10,000gal/hr. The old Pullman depot, which had been vacated when the Pullman company removed its repair works to Brighton, was adapted as a carriage cleaning shed and extended to cover an additional area of 265ft by 150ft. It could accommodate 117 coaches in addition to 46 in the sidings outside. The old goods shed was reconstructed for carriage and wagon repairs and equipped with a workshop and stores. Southern Railway locomotive depots are listed in Table 4.

Table 4 — Southern Railway locomotive depots (1944)

The Southern Railway was eventually divided into two main divisions for locomotive running purposes — Eastern and Western — together with an Isle of Wight Division. Sheds and sub-sheds are listed below:

Eastern Division
Stewarts Lane
Bricklayers Arms
New Cross Gate
  Norwood Junction
Hither Green
Tonbridge
Tunbridge Wells West
Ashford
  Canterbury West
Dover Marine
  Folkestone Jct
Redhill
Gillingham
  Faversham
St Leonards (West Marina)
  Bexhill
  Eastbourne
Ramsgate
Brighton
  Newhaven

Western Division
Nine Elms
Feltham
Guildford
  Bordon
Basingstoke
Fratton
  Gosport
  Midhurst
Horsham
  Three Bridges
Reading
Salisbury
Eastleigh
  Winchester
  Southampton
  Lymington
  Andover Jct
Bournemouth Ctl
  Swanage
  Hamworthy Jct
  Dorchester
Yeovil
  Templecombe
Exmouth Junction
  Seaton
  Lyme Regis
  Exmouth
  Okehampton
  Bude
  Launceston
  Plymouth Friary
  Callington
  Wadebridge
  Barnstaple
  Torrington
  Ilfracombe

Isle of Wight
Ryde
  Newport

SOUTHAMPTON

Perhaps the most impressive development undertaken by the Southern Railway was the £8million Dock Extension Scheme at Southampton. A bay extending for two miles from the Royal Pier to Millbrook Point was reclaimed and along the water front of the area of some 407 acres a quay wall 7,400ft long was built. The length of quay enabled eight of the largest ships of the day to be accommodated at the same time. Eight sheds, each about 900ft long and 150ft wide, were built on the reclaimed land and equipped with the latest machinery for handling cargo and facilities for dealing with passengers.

The scheme included the King George V graving dock, opened by King George V and Queen Mary on 26 July 1933. At that time it was the largest dock of its kind in the world, being 1,200ft long, 165ft wide, and filling to a maximum depth of 45ft of water. These facilities, supported by effective marketing, were instrumental in making Southampton the premier port for trans-Atlantic traffic. A large area of the reclaimed land was sold to Southampton Corporation for municipal purposes, and on another portion an industrial estate was set up.

When it bought the land, the Corporation was assured of improvements to Southampton West station, then consisting of up and down main line platforms and a down bay. Originally Blechynden, the station had been rebuilt in the 1890s and resited west of the Blechynden Road level crossing. In the new reconstruction of 1935 the level crossing was replaced by a concrete and steel overbridge. The old down platform became an island accommodating the down and up through lines. The former up main became the up local platform, and there was a new down local platform with a down bay at its west end. Platform lengths were:

Up local	900ft
Up through	910ft
Down through	910ft
Down local	910ft
Down bay	470ft

New buildings were provided on the down side of the station, including waiting, buffet and tea rooms, using part of the land reclaimed for the docks extension. A new station approach paved with reinforced concrete was built on the same side.

The up side buildings, including a clock tower, were imposing and commodious by the standards of the period when they were built; they were retained, but completely renovated. The station was renamed Southampton Central. At the same time the line was quadrupled from the station to about half-a-mile beyond Millbrook.

WATERLOO & CITY IMPROVEMENT

The Southern Railway took over the Waterloo & City underground railway (1 mile 46ch) connecting Waterloo with the Bank and the London Underground system. It had been built by a separate company in 1898 and acquired by the LSWR in 1907. Thirty years later the original stock was still in service but badly run-down and the subject of numerous complaints. In 1937 it was decided to spend £196,250 on modernisation, to include rolling stock, cables and switchgear, resignalling, and removal of the conductor rail from the centre of the track to the standard position. The new rolling stock was not delivered until 1940. It consisted of 12 motorcoaches (two 190hp motors) and 16 trailers with air-operated doors enabling trains to be operated either as single-cars (one motorcoach) or in formations of two or five cars, the latter comprising two motorcoaches and three trailers. The stock is known today as Class 487.

60
Waterloo & City stock of 1940. *IAL*

5 Electrification

The first electrification of lines that were later to become part of the Southern Railway was in the London area of the LBSCR. Beginning in 1909, the company installed a single-phase ac system with overhead contact wire operating at 6,700V, 25Hz. The LSWR electrified its first London suburban section in 1915 using 600V dc. By 1923 electrification of the SECR London suburban lines, also at 600V dc, was well advanced but the first electric services on that section did not begin until 1925. Routes in operation at Grouping and the dates when public services began are shown in Table 5.

Table 5 SR electrified lines at 1 January 1923

Route	*Date opened*
London Bridge to Victoria via Denmark Hill (South London Line)*	1 December 1909
Victoria to Crystal Palace via Streatham Hill*	12 May 1911
Peckham Rye Junction (South London Line) to Tulse Hill, with connections to the Victoria-Crystal Palace line at Leigham Junction and West Norwood Junction*	1 March 1912
Waterloo-Wimbledon via East Putney	25 October 1915
Waterloo-Malden-Kingston-Richmond-Waterloo; also to Shepperton	30 January 1916
Hounslow loop	12 March 1916
Malden-Hampton Court	18 June 1916
Hampton Court Junction-Claygate	20 November 1916

*6,700V, 25Hz ac. All others are 600V dc

The Railway Centenary year, 1925, saw the first steps in the Southern Railway's own development of suburban electrification. As if to show that the old divisions between companies' territories were to be forgotten, electric services were inaugurated from Waterloo to Dorking North via Raynes Park. Dorking North was an LBSCR station and had previously been served by trains from Victoria or London Bridge only; trains from Waterloo had diverged at Leatherhead to Effingham Junction. The LBSCR and LSWR, although sharing a joint line from Epsom to Leatherhead, had separate stations at both places. From 10 July 1927 all trains used the former LBSC Leatherhead station, a new spur having been built from the 'country' end of that station to join the Effingham Junction line. In 1929 all passenger traffic was concentrated at a new station in Epsom, the former LBSC Epsom Town station being closed.

The other electrification events of 1925 were the first stages of the massive South Eastern Programme, involving extensive engineering works and resignalling at the termini involved; and extension of the ex-LBSC ac overhead system from Balham to Coulsdon North, and to Sutton via Selhurst. The Coulsdon/Sutton project dated from before the war but had been deferred. Work began in 1922 and was in progress at Grouping. Train services were inaugurated on 1 April 1925, but by that time the future of the ac system was in doubt because of the economic and operating problems presented by the existence of two incompatible systems of electrification in Southern Railway territory. After thorough technical investigation the decision was taken in 1926 to standardise 600V dc for future Southern electrification and to convert all the ac lines to that system. The last ac electric trains ran on 22 September 1929, by which time all the former ac lines had been converted for dc working and new sections of the LBSC network had been electrified at 600V dc.

The period from 1923 to 1930 saw fulfilment of the Southern Railway's plans for completing electrification of its London suburban area. With 875 miles of electrified track it could then claim to be 'the world's greatest suburban electrification'. The sections electrified over that period are shown in Table 6.

The ac electric trains for the final phase of the LBSC electrification programme, serving Coulsdon and Sutton, came out with 'Southern Railway' lettering. They were five-car units, the centre vehicle being a motorcoach with luggage space but no passenger seating. The two driving trailers were third class and the other two trailers were composites. Units operated in pairs at peak periods.

The Southern Railway took over 134 vehicles operating on the LBSCR South London and Crystal Palace services. South London Line units consisted originally of two motorcoaches with an intermediate trailer. Driving trailers were later converted from steam stock so that two-coach trains could be run off-peak and six coaches (three two-coach units) in the peak hours. The stock for the Crystal Palace lines consisted of motorcoaches and driving trailers, operated in three-car or six-car formations (increased to eight by a further motorcoach and driving trailer if necessary).

Table 6 SR London Suburban electrification, 1923-30

Route	*Date opened*
Balham-Coulsdon North, and Selhurst-Sutton*	1 April 1925*
Raynes Park-Dorking North; Leatherhead-Effingham Junction; Claygate-Guildford	12 July 1925
Victoria-Herne Hill-Shortlands-Orpington	12 July 1925
Holborn Viaduct-Herne Hill	12 July 1925
Loughborough Junction-Nunhead-Shortlands (Catford Loop)	12 July 1925
Nunhead-Crystal Palace (High Level)	12 July 1925
Charing Cross and Cannon Street to Bromley North, Beckenham Junction, Hayes, Elmers End and Addiscombe	26 February 1926
To Dartford via Greenwich and Woolwich; Blackheath and Woolwich; Bexleyheath; and Sidcup (Dartford Loop)	6 June 1926†
Purley to Caterham and Tattenham Corner; Sydenham to Crystal Palace (Low Level)	25 March 1928‡
Herne Hill-Tulse Hill-Haydons Road-Wimbledon	3 March 1929
Streatham North Junction-Mitcham Junction-Sutton-Epsom	3 March 1929
Sutton-Epsom Downs	17 June 1928
Hounslow and Feltham Junctions to Windsor	6 July 1930
Wimbledon to West Croydon	6 July 1930
Dartford to Gravesend Central	6 July 1930

*Originally 6,700V, 25Hz, single-phase ac. Conversion completed by September 1929.
†A temporary electric service operated between Charing Cross and Dartford from 10 to 16 May 1926 during the General Strike.
‡Temporary service. Full service began 17 June 1928.

South London motorcoaches were powered by four 115hp repulsion motors; those for the Crystal Palace service had four 150hp motors of the same type. By the 1920s, when the Coulsdon/Sutton motorcoaches were built, the single-phase series motor had been fully developed and four 250hp machines of that type were installed. All the ac motorcoaches had bow collectors. The bow is a light mechanically simple device but less suitable than the pantograph for collecting heavy currents. It 'trails' on the wire, and so a separate collector is required for each direction of running. The 1,000hp motorcoaches for the Coulsdon/Sutton services carried four bow collectors so that two could be used at a time.

The LSWR began its electric services with three-coach (motorcoach-trailer-motorcoach) units, each motorcoach powered by two 275hp motors. Units were coupled to form six-coach trains in peak hours. In 1920 some two-coach trailer units were introduced so that eight-coach trains could be formed by coupling a trailer unit between two motor units. Most of this stock was converted from former steam train coaches. For the Southern Railway's Eastern Section electrification of 1925/6, however, new three-coach sets with 300hp motors were ordered from contractors. They were supplemented by conversions of SER steam stock with the same electrical equipment. Two-coach and single-coach trailer units were provided by converting former LBSCR steam-hauled coaches. A further call on ex-LBSC stock was made to provide more motor units for the 1928 electrifications. Similar practices continued up to the new generations of Southern Railway electric rolling stock introduced for the first main line electrifications.

Between 1935 and 1940 the process of lengthening earlier units continued and at the end of the Southern Railway period the latest type of eight-coach set was 515ft long overall, had a seating capacity of 816, and an unladen weight of 285 tons. In such a train there would be four motor bogies and eight 275hp traction motors.

The LBSCR had bought power for its electrifications from the London Electricity Supply Corporation, whose power station was at Deptford. When the LSWR decided to electrify, however, it built its own power station at Durnsford Road, Wimbledon, beginning construction in July 1913. The boiler house contained 16 Babcock & Wilcox boilers supplying steam at 200lb/sq in to five 5,000kW Dick, Kerr turbo-alternators. Three-phase current was generated at 11,000V, 25Hz, and transmitted to substations where rotary-converters changed it to 600V dc for the live rails. The sub-standard frequency of 25Hz was

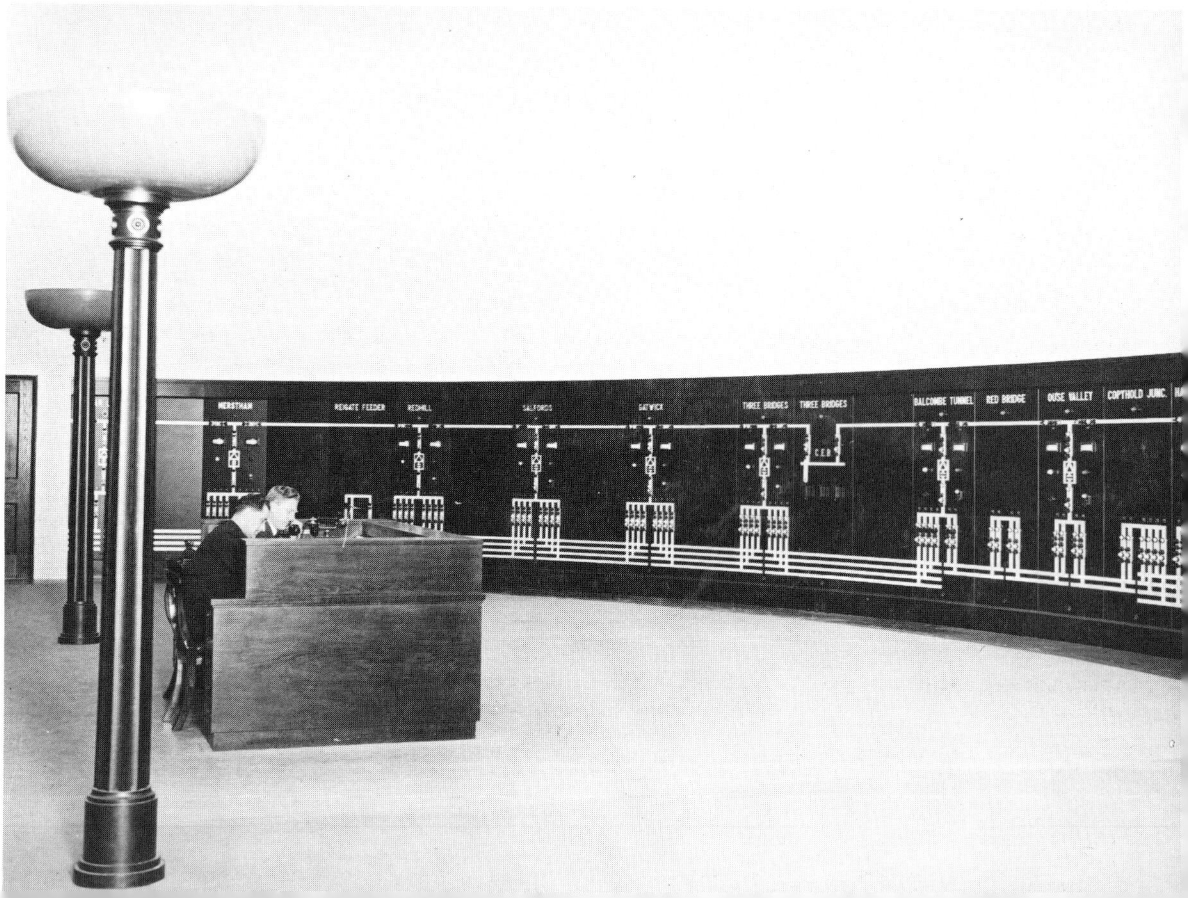

MERSTHAM
REIGATE FEEDER
REDHILL
SALFORDS
GATWICK
THREE BRIDGES
THREE BRIDGES
C.E.B.
BALCOMBE TUNNEL
RED BRIDGE
OUSE VALLEY
COPTHOLD JUNC.

61
A motor luggage van for the Sutton/Coulsdon electrification. One of the bow collectors for the opposite direction of running can be seen lowered at the nearer end of the vehicle. *H. C. Casserley*

adopted because the rotary converters of that period had problems in handling a standard industrial frequency (50Hz) supply.

The SECR also proposed to generate its own power but its application to build a power station at Angerstein Wharf, Charlton, was turned down by the Electricity Commissioners. The supply was therefore taken from the London Electricity Supply Corporation at 11,000V, 25Hz, three-phase, and distributed to rotary-converter sub-stations.

Substations with rotary converting plant at first had to be manned, but by the time of the Southern's Dorking/Guildford electrification of 1925 unmanned substations under remote control were coming into use. In that scheme the substations at Leatherhead and Clandon were controlled from the new substation at Effingham Junction, and that at Oxshott from the existing substation at Hampton Court Junction. At the same time the static mercury-arc rectifier for traction was on the horizon. When Sir Herbert Walker, General Manager of the Southern Railway, announced to a meeting of his officers in 1929, 'Gentlemen, I have decided to electrify to Brighton', there is little doubt that these technical developments were in his mind.

Electrification of the Brighton line had already reached Coulsdon, only 36 miles from the coast. The decision to extend to the coast was announced to Southern Railway shareholders at the annual general meeting in February 1930. In addition to the main line to Brighton, the coast line from Brighton to West Worthing was to be electrified, together with the Cliftonville curve from Preston Park to Hove which by-passed the terminal station at Brighton for Worthing trains. While the work was in progress colour-light signalling was being installed between Coulsdon and Brighton, replacing semaphores. The resignalling was completed in the autumn of 1932 and gave the Southern Railway the longest continuous stretch of colour-light signalling in the country.

When the LBSCR undertook electrification to Coulsdon the Redhill-Reading line was still SECR territory and so Reigate, the first station out of Redhill, continued to be served by steam trains.The Southern Railway's Brighton line electrification included the two miles from Redhill to Reigate, to the benefit of Reigate commuters.

Power for the electrification was taken from the Central Electricity Board at Croydon, Three Bridges and Fishergate (near Hove), and distributed over lineside cables to 18 substations. All substations were equipped with mercury-arc rectifiers and operated under remote supervisory control from a control room at Three Bridges. The electrification was opened in two stages, as shown in Table 7, which lists in chronological order the Southern Railway's electrification schemes outside the London area from 1932 to 1939.

62
Three Bridges control room for the Brighton electrification. The diagram panels show the connections at substations from Merstham to Haywards Heath, and the Reigate feeder point. *BR*

Table 7 Main line and outer suburban electrifications*

Route	*Opened*
Coulsdon-Three Bridges; and Redhill-Reigate	17 July 1932
Three Bridges-Brighton, Hove and West Worthing	1 January 1933
Bickley Junction-St Mary Cray	1 May 1934
St Mary Cray-Sevenoaks via Swanley Junction	6 January 1935
Orpington-Sevenoaks	6 January 1935
Haywards Heath to Lewes, Seaford, Eastbourne, Hastings and Ore; Haywards Heath-Horsted Keynes; Brighton-Lewes	7 July 1935
Nunhead-Lewisham	30 September 1935
Woodside-Sanderstead	30 September 1935
Staines-Weybridge	3 January 1937
Hampton Court Junction-Woking, Guildford, Havant and Portsmouth; Woking-Alton	4 July 1937
Dorking North and Three Bridges-Horsham; Horsham-Ford; West Worthing-Ford, Chichester, Havant	3 July 1938
Virginia Water-Reading; Ascot-Ash Vale; Frimley Junction-Sturt Lane Junction and Pirbright Junction; Aldershot North Junction-Guildford	1 January 1939
Gravesend Central-Strood-Maidstone West (including spur from Strood to main line at Rochester Bridge Junction)	2 July 1939
Swanley-Gillingham (Kent)	2 July 1939
Otford-Maidstone East	2 July 1939

*The Motspur Park-Chessington branch in the London suburban area was electrified in this period, opening to Tolworth on 29 May 1938 and to Chessington South on 28 May 1939

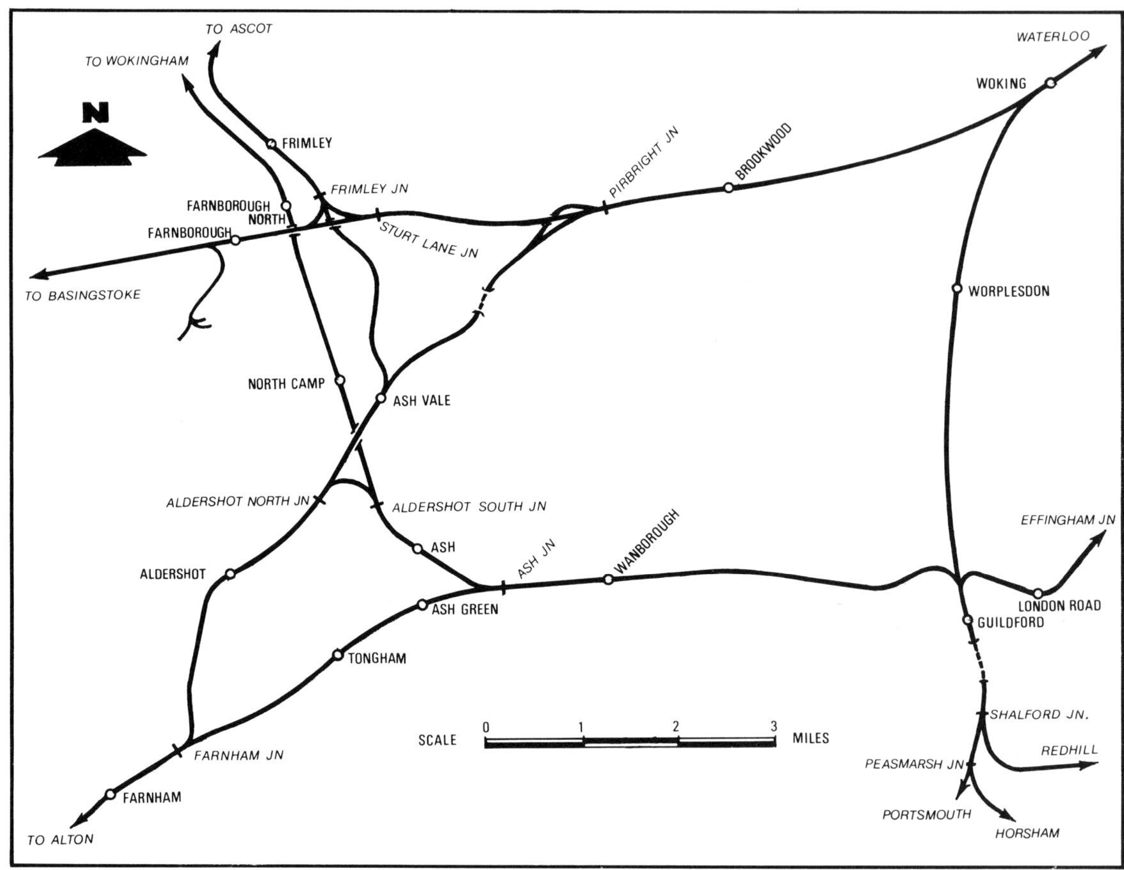

Fig 7
Junctions in the Farnborough/Aldershot/Guildford area

Junctions in the Aldershot-Guildford area covered by the Reading electrification of 1 January 1939 are shown in Fig 7.

With the Brighton main line electrification a new generation of multiple-unit stock was launched. Brighton fast trains were formed of six-car units, each including a two-class Pullman car and designated 6PUL. The make-up was as follows:

Third class centre-gangway motorcoach (four 225hp motors)
Composite trailer (side corridor)
Pullman car
Composite trailer (side corridor)
Third class trailer (side corridor)
Motorcoach (as above)

Units were gangwayed throughout, but there was no communication between them. However, with a Pullman car in each half of a 12-car train all passengers had access to refreshments.

Three sets were built with three first class trailers to cater for the high proportion of first class season ticket holders on the 'City Limited' and were accordingly classified '6-CITY'.

The all-Pullman 5BEL sets for the 'Brighton Belle' service consisted of two third class motor cars (four 225hp motors each), a third class 'parlour car' and two first class cars with kitchen and pantry.

Semi-fast services were worked by four-car units (4LAV) consisting of:

Third class non-corridor motorcoach (two 275hp motors)
Non-corridor composite trailer
Side-corridor composite trailer, 2 lavatories
Motorcoach as above

At first LSW-type three-car sets were employed on stopping services but in 1934 the 2NOL class units were ready. Each consisted of a composite motorcoach (two 275hp motors) and a composite driving trailer, both without corridor.

More six-car units were built for the Eastbourne/Hastings express services. Power equipment was similar to the 6PULs but a first class compartment coach with pantry for serving refreshments replaced the Pullman car. These units worked with the 6PULs, the usual formation for all South Coast expresses being 6PUL/6PAN.

The semi-fast units for Eastbourne/Hastings were the 2BILs. These two-car sets were not vestibuled but each vehicle had a side corridor and lavatory. Motorcoaches, with two 275hp motors, were third class, and the driving trailers composites.

Portsmouth No 1 brought a change of practice. The fast trains were made up of four-car units with corridor connections at the ends so that when two or more units were coupled, passengers could walk from end to end of the train and all had access to a restaurant car. The driving compartments were of reduced width to allow for the gangway, and the headcode was displayed where the right hand cab window would normally have been. This gave the trains a 'one-eyed' appearance which was said to have inspired the nickname 'Nelsons'. Officially they were 4CORS and had the following make-up:

Open third motorcoach (two 225hp motors)
Compartment composite
Compartment third
Motorcoach (as above)

There were similar sets with restaurant cars (4RES), the trailers being a first class car with four com-

63
A 6PUL/6PAN formation, complete with destination boards, passes New Cross Gate in the early days of the Brighton electrification. London Bridge services had odd-number headcodes. *H. N. James*

64
The 'Brighton Belle' formed of two 5BEL units passes Haywards Heath at speed. *C. P. Boocock*

65
Semi-fast services on the Brighton line were provided by the 4LAV sets. No 2948 (renumbered) is at Redhill.
P. J. Sharpe

66
The 2BIL units were introduced for semi-fast services on the Eastbourne/Hastings electrification. More were built for the Mid-Sussex scheme (Portsmouth via Horsham) and unit No 2061 of the class heads a train at Havant on the west coast line.

partments and open dining section; and a third class car with kitchen, pantry and open dining section.

The traction motors in these units had finned frames to improve cooling on the long grades of the 'direct Portsmouth' line. It will be noted that the total power of a 4COR or 4RES was 900hp, or half that of a 6-coach unit on the Brighton or Eastbourne/Hastings services, and in spite of lower unit weight there was little margin for time recovery. Klapper in *Sir Herbert Walker's Southern Railway* (see bibliography) relates how on a demonstration run Alfred Raworth, the company's Chief Electrical Engineer, repeated several times 'These motors are just right', perhaps to convince himself after doubts on their adequacy had been raised. In practice, however, they stood up well to their work, demonstrating the remarkable overload capacity of electrical machines for short periods even in those days of less advanced insulating materials.

More 4COR units were built for the Portsmouth No 2 scheme, together with 4BUF units in which a buffet car replaced the compartment third. O. V. S. Bulleid was now in change of motive power and rolling stock, and the buffets bore an individualistic imprint. The bar section had no windows, perhaps foreshadowing the Tavern Cars of future years, although these conceded shallow elongated slits above eye level. In the refreshment section the tables faced the windows and their inner edge had a concave curve opposite each of the revolving seats, not to accommodate corpulence but to allow the seats to be 'inset' so as to leave an adequate gangway between their backs. The same concave curvature was seen in the series of cusps forming the arch of interior partitions and door frames.

More two-coach units were built for the electrified services to Maidstone and Gillingham introduced in the summer of 1939. The motorcoaches had two 275hp motors as in the 2BIL sets but were non-corridor. The trailers were composites with a side corridor and lavatory. This feature earned them the classification 2HAL ('Half-Lavatory' compared with the provision in the 2BILs of one lavatory per coach).

Only two types of traction motor were in use — suburban and express. Both types were totally enclosed and axle-hung. The characteristics were as below:

	Suburban	*Express*
Normal average accelerating current up to 26.5mph (4-coach unit)	410A	310A
Rate of acceleration (4-coach unit) mph/sec	1.0	0.5
Balancing speed (4-coach unit)	55mph	64.5mph
1hr rating at 600V	275hp	225hp
Max safe speed	75mph	85mph
Gear ratio	2.81:1	2.48:1

The motors were controlled by series/parallel switching, with 11 resistance steps during acceleration. In four-motor motorcoaches each pair of motors was switched separately. Control equipment was electromagnetic at first, the contactor coils being energised from the live rail supply. From 1932 electro-pneumatic equipment was installed and the coils were energised at 70V from a tapping on a potentiometer. Weights and horsepower of the various units introduced from the beginning of the main-line electrifications are shown in Table 8.

Table 8 SR mainline electric units

Class	*Weights* *Unit*		*Motor-coach*		*Total hp (1hr)*
	T	C	T	C	
2-coach non-corridor, no lav (2NOL)	72	10	42	10	550
2-coach corridor & 2 lav. (2BIL)	74	2	43	5	550
2-coach, 1 corridor & 1 lav (2HAL)	74	1	43	1	550
4-coach, 1 corridor 1 lav, (4LAV)	139	0	41	0	1,100
4-coach express corridor. (4COR)	158	5	46	10	900
4-coach express kitchen corridor. (4RES)	161	8	46	10	900
4-coach express buffet corridor. (4BUF)	162	14	46	10	900
5-coach express all-Pullman. (5BEL)	250	11	62	8	1,800
6-coach express with Pullman. (6PUL)	265	9	59	0	1,800

In 1947, the last year of the Southern Railway, the Southern Electric system totalled 709miles 23ch. In the London area power supplies for the Western Section were taken from the Southern's own power station at Durnsford Road, Wimbledon; and for the Central and Eastern Sections from the Deptford East power station of the London Electricity Supply Corporation. Durnsford Road fed 17 substations. Power from Deptford East was distributed via Lewisham to 29 substations. Both these supplies were at 11kV, 25Hz, and all substations on the 11kV systems were equipped with rotary converters; 42 of them were attended and 4 unattended.

Durnsford Road in 1947 had 20 boilers with a total evaporation of 430,000lb/hr, and 6 turbo-alternator sets, 2 of 5MW and 4 of 12.5MW.

Outside the London area supplies at 33kV, 50Hz, were taken from the national Grid system and fed into a ring main supplying 113 substations, all equipped with mercury-arc rectifiers and unattended. A pumpless air-cooled rectifier was installed at Purley in 1942 but the remainder were water-cooled, with pumps to maintain the vacuum. At substations the rectifiers were connected to the busbars through circuit-breakers rated to carry 4,000A which tripped if a rectifier fault allowed reverse current to flow. The busbars were connected to the conductor rails through high-speed circuit-breakers rated to carry 2,500A continuously and opening in 0.01sec in the event of a fault. At track-paralleling huts between substations there were gaps in the conductor rails, bridged by busbars in the huts to which rails were connected by similar circuit-breakers. They ensured that wherever a train might be when a fault occurred in its equipment it would be close enough to a circuit-breaker to effect immediate interruption of the supply.

The supply system outside the London area was monitored and controlled from five control rooms, from which all circuit-breakers could be opened if it was necessary to isolate a section of track in an

67
A down Portsmouth express formed of 4COR units approaches Clapham Junction. *C. C. B. Herbert*

68
Unit No 3083 was one of the 4BUF sets built for the Bognor/Portsmouth fast trains via the Mid-Sussex line. It is seen here at Arundel on an up service to Victoria.
P. J. Sharpe

emergency or for maintenance. These centres, with the number of substations and track paralleling huts controlled from each are tabulated below:

Centre	*Substations*	*Track paralleling huts*
Woking	30	23
Three Bridges	31	14
Havant	26	25
Swanley	21	19
Ore	5	4

The final step in Southern Railway traction development was the introduction of the lightweight self-ventilated motor in 1947. This machine had a tapped field. On full field it reproduced the performance of the standard suburban motor, and on weak-field that of the express motor. The previous totally-enclosed motors had heavy frames to dissipate heat. In the self-ventilated machine a fan on the armature shaft drew air through the motor, which improved the cooling and allowed the use of a lighter frame. The weight of the lightweight motor was only 1.92 tons, compared with 3.38 tons of the earlier express machine, and 3.6 tons of the suburban motor.

69
The 'Arabian Nights' interior of a Mid-Sussex 4BUF showing the curvaceous bar counter and revolving-top stools. *BR*

6 The Southern Image

From the latitude of London northwards it is almost a traditional belief that the South Coast and the area behind it is a land of sunshine. The belief was being fostered by interested parties long before the days of the Southern Railway. Among early writings on Brighton there is a poem of humorous protest by a visitor who had gone there expecting a Costa del Sol but had instead been alternately buffeted by wind and lashed with rain. However, the idea persisted and the Southern Railway was quick to take advantage of it. One of its first posters was the famous one showing a small boy with a suitcase talking to the driver of a Urie 4-6-0 at the end of one of the Waterloo platforms, with the legend 'For holidays I always go Southern 'cos its the Sunshine Line'.

The original of the poster was a snapshot which is said to have been sent originally to the Publicity Department of the LSWR. It was first put to use by the Southern Railway, and according to one report the first letters of the word 'Southern' were added to the visible portion of the locomotive tender. By the time the poster was produced there was no record of the boy's identity. The Southern tried to trace him, offering a framed copy of the poster in which he appeared, and several parents presented children whom they claimed to be the boy. They were disqualified when it became apparent that they assumed the original photograph to have been taken a short time before, whereas SR Publicity knew its origin to have been a year or more earlier. When the boy was at length traced he was found to be Wilfred Witt, son of a former employee in the Electrical Engineer's Department who had emigrated to California. So Wilfred had found his sunshine, though not on the Sunshine Line.

The Witt poster appeared in 1925. Five years later the Southern launched a character who was to become as closely associated with it as the dancing fisherman with the resort of Skegness. This was 'Sunny South Sam', portrayed as 'a cheery and typical Southern Railway guard'. His genial countenance appeared on innumerable posters advertising cheap fares and other facilities. The original model was Harry Tilbury, a Lancashire man and actor, who was chosen because he was 'the friendly type of person to whom people would like to write about their holidays'. Unhappily, Tilbury died only two months after the first 'Sunny South Sam' posters went on display. They were all removed, or his portrait was blanked out, but a successor had been chosen and soon 'Sunny South Sam' became a household name.

70
The Southern Railway's best-known poster.
Crown Copyright National Railway Museum, York

71
'Sunny South Sam' spreads the 'South for Sunshine' message.
Crown Copyright National Railway Museum, York

There was a minor flutter in 1939 when the London & North Eastern Railway, not content with its 'Drier Side of Britain' slogan, launched a 'Meet the Sun on the East Coast' campaign. The Southern reacted swiftly with a poster showing Meteorological Office figures to prove that 26 out of 32 resorts with the best sunshine figures were served by the Southern Railway. They followed up with a 'Facts about Sunshine' poster, and one headed 'Set Fair on the South Coast' in which the coastline was represented as the trace on a barograph chart. Sunny South Sam featured in the campaign, drawing attention to the Southern's holiday brochures *Hints for Holidays* and *Sands across the Sea*.

The Southern also issued posters of its 'King Arthur' and 'Lord Nelson' class locomotives, and during the electrifications of the 1930s portrayed its electric trains in attractive settings. A Portsmouth train of 4-COR units near Rowlands Castle was a particularly effective essay in this style. Apart from these and similar posters with a direct railway appeal there were many others emphasising the attractions of the area it served, both for holidays and for residence. 'Live in Surrey free from worry' and 'Live in Kent and be content' were slogans that tempted many to move away from the London suburbs.

In its early days the Southern Railway was given a rough ride by the Press. The campaign of complaints had an unlooked-for outcome. Although his instincts were to keep his plans to himself, Sir Herbert Walker, the General Manager, saw the need for contacts with the newspapers. He decided that the best man to talk to the Press would be one who knew from personal experience how the Press thought and reacted. He found such a man in John Elliot, who had seen public relations in practice in the United States and had experience of journalism in the USA and Britain. Elliot was appointed Assistant for Public Relations on the General Manager's staff on 16 January 1925, becoming the first holder on a British railway of the now familiar PRO title. His later involvement on the operating side led him to the top. He became Deputy General Manager of the Southern Railway in 1939, and was Acting General Manager at the time of nationalisation.

Although Sir Herbert Walker's first approach to public relations had been cautious, his interest in promoting the public image of the Southern Railway grew rapidly. His officers, too, understood the publicity value of attractive colour schemes for locomotives and coaches, and in March 1936 *The Railway Magazine* reported that 'one of the standard multiple-unit express electric sets as used on the Brighton and Eastbourne trains of the Southern Railway is now running painted a vivid green'. In his book *Sir Herbert Walker's Southern Railway* the late Charles F. Klapper relates an anecdote of a visit to the Isle of Wight by Sir Herbert Walker and some of his officers in 1936. On the way down to Portsmouth Walker listened quietly while questions of livery were discussed. Later in the day, while the party was passing an optician's shop in Portsmouth, Walker suddenly darted inside and emerged with a reel of coloured spectacle cord, from which he cut a length to give to each officer. As he made the distribution he said: 'Now, argument shall cease; that will be the colour Southern engines and coaches shall be painted in future. This reel shall remain in my office safe as the standard to which reference shall be made'. Klapper was told the story by a member of the party. Walker retired in 1937 a fortnight before O. V. S. Bulleid became Chief Mechanical Engineer and responsible for liveries. It is not known whether Walker's 'standard' reel was still in his safe, or whether Bulleid referred to it in choosing the malachite green livery associated today with his name.

Early in its history the Southern Railway gave practical proof in new station buildings of the importance it attached to its public image. In 1926 the new Ramsgate station set the theme. In *Railway Stations, Southern Region* (see bibliography) the authors comment that the buildings at Ramsgate 'while very much of their period retain the feeling of solid and fairly prosperous respectability associated with the pre-1914 era, but they begin to show the importance which the Southern Railway continued to attach to the main entrance and booking hall as dominant features in external design'. The 1930s saw a new era, and reconstructions of stations at Haywards Heath, Kingston, Surbiton and Horsham 'retain the principal points of emphasis in the earlier buildings but reject the tiled roof and the arched opening in seeking a modern transport "image" more consistent with the extremely progressive and successful "Southern Electric" '.

72
Admirers of a later generation gather round 'Merchant Navy' Pacific No 21C13 *Blue Funnel* waiting to leave Waterloo with the 'Bournemouth Belle'. *F. G. Reynolds*

73
The concrete style of the rebuilt station at Surbiton recalls the Super Cinema facades of the period. *BR*

74
Exeter Queen Street station in LSWR days. *LPC/IAL*

75
The Southern Railway rebuilt Queen Street as Exeter Central. This view was taken in the early nationalisation years. *John Robertson*

As late as 1933 the Southern was also employing a 'civic' style. When the new Exeter Central station was opened in that year, replacing the old Queen Street, the main building at street level was set back in a crescent form, fronted by a paved forecourt. *The Railway Gazette* commented that 'the main block stands up in conscious dignity and is set off on each side by concave-sweeping two-storeyed buildings which seem a little uncertain of themselves, as do poor relations in the presence of an opulent member of the family. About this main block there is not a trace of uncertainty, in terms of brick and stone it proclaims itself as a citizen of no mean city and with justifiable complacency it takes its place among the other buildings of Exeter'. Some had said that it might be mistaken for a town hall or a public library, but *The Railway Gazette* stoutly maintained that it looked like a railway station; otherwise it would not have 'the words "Southern Railway" upon the frieze of its entablature'.

The up platform at Queen Street had been lengthened in 1925 to take two trains simultaneously. In the new station the track layout was modified with the down platform lengthened. The former all-over roof and buildings were demolished, new umbrella awnings erected on the platforms, and the platforms were connected by that Southern hallmark, a reinforced concrete footbridge.

The Southern's shareholders were kept informed of the company's thinking in this direction. At the annual general meeting in 1938 the Chairman, Mr R. Holland Martin, said: 'In our new stations such as Surbiton and Richmond we have endeavoured to provide cheerful, clean and businesslike structures capable of dealing expeditiously with our ever-increasing traffic with comfort to the passenger, for we find that improved stations bring increased revenue'. Work was in hand at that period with remodelling on similar lines at Woking, Templecombe, Swanage and other stations, while Twickenham was shortly to be reconstructed as were Horsham, Littlehampton and Chichester.

A foretaste of the 'concrete phase' in Southern station architecture was given in 1929 by the new facade at Wimbledon. *The Railway Gazette* reported that 'the exterior finish is white concrete and the words "Southern Railway" effectively set out in white lettering with green edging and measuring about 2ft in height are carried above the centre entrance'. A sign over the awning read: 'Southern Electric and Underground trains to all parts of London and to Hampton Court, Kingston, etc'. The Southern inherited its interest in concrete from the London & South Western Railway which had established a concrete depot at Exmouth Junction in 1913 for manufacturing pre-cast concrete items for use throughout the system. The depot was enlarged by the SR and new designs were introduced. In the 1930s the articles produced at Exmouth Junction ranged from boundary posts to large single-storey buildings and bridges. The buildings were built up of standard sections and ranged from fogmen's shelters to large warehouses. Footbridges were also of sectional construction; the longest was at Seaton Junction with eight spans and an overall length of 300ft. The output of the depot was 2,000 articles a week, many of them, of course, being small items such as mileposts, gradient posts, trestles for carrying signal wires and point rodding, and fencing posts. The depot also produced concrete fencing and various types of platform walling, and such items distributed all over the system gave a coherent Southern 'look' to railway installations in environments as different as inner London suburbs and the far West Country. 'Can it really be that this same carriage came from Waterloo' mused John Betjeman en route to Wadebridge. Perhaps a line of concrete posts or a platelayer's hut that might just as well have stood at Walton-on-Thames assured him that it did.

But some old images derived from its constituent companies still haunted the Southern Railway in its early years. In August 1926 the railway put out an official announcement deprecating the continuing use of the old company names. It said: 'The old terms "South Western", "Brighton" and "South Eastern" have not been in official use for some time, the correct designations being Western Section, Central Section, and Eastern Section . . . No good purpose is served by perpetuating the idea of the three separate companies now that they are amalgamated and under one control'. As evidence of its unifying efforts, the railway pointed to the fact that the platforms at Victoria were now numbered continuously from 1 to 17 and stated that new departure indicators under construction at the time would show departures for the whole station. Just as the physical separation between the Brighton and South Eastern sides was broken down at Victoria, so it was at London Bridge where direct access was provided from the ex-LBSC terminal platforms to the through platforms on the South Eastern side of the station.

New train services reflected the same unifying trend, such as Waterloo to Dorking North, which had been LBSC territory and served only from Victoria or London Bridge. But tradition was still respected where it involved a popular public facility and when the 'Southern Belle' attained its majority on 1 November 1929 the 'birthday' run to Brighton behind 'King Arthur' 4-6-0 No E793, *Sir Ontzlake*, was followed by lunch for the railway's guests at the Royal Albion Hotel. The train had run to a 60min schedule for 21 years and was to continue to do so, but now with 10 or 11 cars weighing up to 400 tons compared with the

76
Main line electrification brought much rebuilding of stations, of which Horsham is an example. *IAL*

77
In earlier years the Southern had sometimes chosen a 'town hall' style, as at Southampton West with its once famous clock tower. *IAL*

original seven-car formation weighing 208 tons. It may have been felt that no acceleration of a world-famous service in 21 years did not contribute much lustre to the Southern image, for an official pronouncement was at pains to justify the policy. A speaker at the luncheon explained: 'Although with more powerful locomotives it would be possible to cut this time slightly . . . it is believed that the wiser policy is to retain an already fast schedule, which on 99 occasions out of 100 can be rigidly kept in all weathers and even under adverse circumstances, rather than to cut the time by a few minutes and so reduce the margin as to make it impossible to maintain the high degree of day-to-day punctuality which has earned the 'Southern Belle' its enviable reputation'. In these last days of steam to Brighton 13 or 14 services covered the distance between London and Brighton in 60min and 'in the morning and evening rush hours the railway gave an express service which for speed and frequency combined, was probably unique in the world'.

To a large proportion of rail travellers in Southern England, however, the predominant feature of the Southern Railway was its electrification. As General Manager of the London & South Western, Sir Herbert Walker had put his faith in electric traction for suburban services. This was not just because of the operating advantages of the multiple-unit train in quick turn-round, rapid acceleration and elimination of locomotive movements at busy terminals. Such things are scarcely noticed by the travelling public, but the pattern of train service is very important to them. Walker aimed at frequent trains and regular intervals. He is reported to have said 'people don't like timetables' and he wanted the public to be confident that on going to any Southern Electric station they would catch a train without a long wait. He thought 15min quite long enough to wait for a train even in the days when competition from the private car was less intense. These ideas were inherent in the planning of the Southern Electric timetable both for local services and the later main line routes, and provided convenient connections where a change of train was necessary. Similar principles are being applied today to inter-city services on the Continent and under such intriguing names as *Taktfahrplan* and *Neue Reisezugkonsept* attract admiring comment such as was rarely earned by the homely British product.

The Southern was able to present a more glamorous image than emus shuttling to and fro in the Home Counties. Boat trains from Victoria were the link with the international expresses of Continental Europe, a fact often emphasised in the company's publicity. Headed by an 'Arthur' or a 'Nelson', its carriage headboards proclaiming it as a Continental Express, the Southern Railway boat train of the 1920s and 1930s stirred the imagination. It was a reassuring start to what was then to many the novelty of a trip across the Channel, and a symbol of the solidity and excellence of British institutions on the return.

Apart from the image promoted by its own efforts, a railway acquires one from the territory it serves. The Southern was always associated with the sea and this in itself gained it the affection of an island race. The young traveller to Bournemouth on holiday had a glimpse after Southampton West of the 'great steamers white and gold' which had been the subject of verses learned in the classroom. Naval traffic to Portsmouth, Chatham and Devonport was a reminder of the British role in maintaining the freedom of the seas. The Southern map showed its tracks closely following coastline and estuary, or putting out short branches to delectable resorts. It longest western tentacle found its way at last to the Atlantic shore.

78
A Southern Railway poster linking the railway with the prestige of the big ships of the 1930s. *BR*

Sherlock Holmes once rebuked Dr Watson with the words 'You *see*, Watson, but you do not *observe*'. The present writer 'saw' that Southern Railway locomotives and coaches were green but is unwilling to commit himself further. Fortunately others observed more acutely. Their works are recorded in the bibliography, and the following notes are based on their researches.

The first Southern green was the sage green used by Urie on the LSWR. It was soon superseded by Maunsell's shade, which has been described as 'darker and bluer'. Passenger locomotives in this colour had white lining with black edging, and chrome yellow lettering and numerals. Bufferbeams were unlined red. Locomotive nameplates in 1925 had raised, polished letters on a dark green background although the background of nameplates of LBSC locomotives was vermilion. In 1936 vermilion was adopted as the background for numberplates.

Goods locomotives were black with dark green lining, later changed in some classes to emerald green.

The standard coach livery was Maunsell green sides, orange lining with black edging, black ends, underframes and bogies (driving ends of electric stock were green). In 1929 many steam and electric coaches appeared in a very dark green when repainted.

In 1936 the passenger locomotive livery was Brunswick green lined out with black and white. A year later the standard livery for Southern locomotives was described as a ' "middle green" inclining to olive shade above the footplate' (Walker's spectacle cord, perhaps?).

Malachite green, which Haresnape (see bibliography) sees as Bulleid's own choice, first appeared in 1938 on the buffet cars built for the Portsmouth No 2 electrification; in the same year it was applied to steam stock and to express engines. Lining was golden yellow with black edging. Goods engines were unlined black.

At the end of 1939 it was announced officially that a decision on a standard livery was in abeyance. Some engines and coaching stock were appearing at that time in the old olive yellow green shade, but unlined. In 1941 all but 150 of the company's steam engines were painted black. This style, unlined, became the wartime livery, with yellow numbers and letters shaded malachite green with a yellow highlight. From 1946 the locomotive livery was malachite green, unlined. Coaching stock remained basically as prewar, but malachite green, without lining, replaced Maunsell green for general utility vans, Post Office coaches and livestock vans.

Stations, buildings and fittings also struck a coherent Southern note. Light green was used for roofing steelwork (under awnings, etc) and ornamental brackets. Notice boards had a 4in dark green border and grey centre, mid-chrome green was the colour of awning columns, railings, handrails, lamp posts, most metal fittings, internal walls (up to 4ft from the floor but deep cream above), window frames and doors. Dark stone colour was used for external valances, signalbox wooden planking and balustrades, wooden hut exteriors, some gates and close-boarded fences. Most signs were green and white, but warnings were red and white. Water tanks, ladders, water columns and signalbox walkways were grey.

The Southern did not confine its image-building to inanimate objects. Staff were required to play their part. The company's clothing schedule laid it down that 'Station masters and other members of the Supervisory Staff supplied with clothing should at all times appear in their proper and complete uniform and also see that the staff under their control observe the same rule'. Trousers were to be properly braced and turn-ups were not permitted. Ties had to be worn by staff when on duty; four were supplied to all entitled at the summer issue of clothing. The LSWR red tie was extended to other Sections, beginning with the Eastern Section as from 1 May 1924. The official announcement explained that the tie could be used as a danger signal by day, and 'by placing a protected light under the red necktie, by night also'.

There were various types of badges. The gilt badge with the letters 'SR' and laurel wreath was reserved for the grades of Station Master, Traffic Controller, Yard Master, and Relief Clerk. The stationmaster's annual uniform issue was '1 jacket (DB), 1 vest (body), 2 trousers, 1 cap, 1 badge'. Overcoats were replaced every two years, 'with velvet collar for special class'. Caps came in 15 patterns. By 1930 hats were among the items only issued to those who had drawn uniform before 19 August 1916. In this section the Schedule showed 'hats, 2' but with the note that this applied only to the stationmasters at Victoria and Brighton. Presumably they were 'hats (top)'.

The electric motorman was distinguished from the steam locomotive driver by being issued with a 'jacket (DB)'. Steam drivers and firemen received a 'jacket (SB)' but they also had two overall coats and the choice of an overcoat or reefer every two years, which were not available to the motorman. Otherwise all these men had the same annual entitlement of 1 vest, body; 2 trousers, 4 ties, 1 cap, and 1 badge (the driver's and fireman's was specified as metal and renewed as necessary).

A tight rein was kept on sartorial matters. A warning notice on the first page read: 'This schedule sets forth in detail the standard supply of Uniform Clothing and protective clothing to the various grades in each Department, and no alteration in pattern or quality is to be made, or any additional garment provided, without the authority of the Directors or General Manager being first obtained'.

7 Train Services

The Southern Railway public timetable was a *Bradshaw* format publication selling for six old pence. Maps were contained in a pocket at the back, one of them showing the suburban system with an index to stations and a grid reference for finding them. Principal internal and Continental services were summarised on coloured pages at the beginning of the book. A pre-Grouping feature that lingered on until 1932 was slip carriage working on the Central (ex-LBSC) Section. The timetable column of the 5.05pm from London Bridge to Horsham via Crawley carried the note 'Carriages for Forest Row slipped at Horley'. They were taken forward calling at all stations and reached Forest Row at 6.20pm (1929 timetable). On Saturdays a slip service to Forest Row was provided by the 5.20pm Victoria-Eastbourne, the carriages being slipped at Three Bridges and reaching Forest Row at 6.34pm.

Brighton also had a slip service, a portion being slipped from the 5.08pm from London Bridge to Worthing, which ran non-stop to Preston Park. The Brighton coaches were slipped at Haywards Heath and called at all stations from there. Slips at Beckenham, Swanley and Faversham were inherited by the Southern from the SECR and continued in operation until 1926.

Steam trains to Littlehampton travelled via Worthing like the present electric service or via the Mid-Sussex line. The best of them was the 6.20pm from Victoria which in 1930 ran non-stop to Horsham via Crawley and reached Littlehampton at 7.55pm. A seasonal service from Victoria at 10.08am on Mondays, Fridays and Saturdays travelled via Sutton and arrived Littlehampton at 12.01pm, and there was a daily train from London Bridge at 10.30am, routed via Crawley and arriving at 12.35pm.

On the Eastern Section the 80min Charing Cross-Folkestone trains (stopping only at Waterloo SECR) were a prestige service and the reason for the design of the 'L1' class 4-4-0s, but they were not numerous. In 1930 there were two in each direction, at 4.15 and 7.15pm from Charing Cross, and at 11.10am and 5.00pm from Folkestone. The fastest pre-Grouping time had been 83min by a service from Cannon Street. By 1938 a Saturdays Only service from Charing Cross at 12.55pm had been added to the 80min trains but ran non-stop, and there was a fast up service at 9.10am which called only at Shorncliffe and reached London Bridge in 78min and according to the public timetable terminated there.

The South Eastern & Chatham was running from Victoria to Margate in 90min in 1914 and in 1921 put on a Sundays Only all-Pullman train, the 'Thanet Limited' with this timing. The Pullman service continued under the Southern with the same timing and in the 1930 timetables carried the note 'Thanet Limited cars' but the proportion of Pullmans to ordinary stock had declined and eventually there were only one or two in the formation to provide refreshment service. In his review of fastest daily times from London in *The Railway Magazine* of April 1939 the late Cecil J. Allen noted the London-Margate service as one of those 'of which the best times are level with but no better than those of 1914'.

Principal trains on the London-Margate-Ramsgate service as shown in the summary pages of the Southern's 1930 summer timetable were as below:

									Suns
Victoria	dep	8.55	10.34	11.24S	3.15			7.00	10.00P
Cannon Street	dep					5.06	6.08		
Margate	arr	10.58	12.50	1.27	4.42	6.39	8.10	9.00	11.30
Ramsgate	arr	11.20	1.13	1.49	5.13	7.01	8.10	9.23	11.52
Ramsgate	dep	7.25	7.33	8.30	10.05	2.00	2.45S	5.05	6.45P
Margate	dep	7.42	7.48	8.47	10.25	2.18	3.04	5.30	7.00
Cannon Street	arr	9.23	9.36	10.32	12.10	4.29	4.05		
Victoria	arr			10.32	12.10	4.29	4.54	7.10	8.30

S = Saturdays Only
P = 'Thanet Limited' cars

79
'L1' class 4-4-0 No 787 with an SECR 'birdcage' brake behind the tender and Pullman car further back presents the typical aspect of Southern Railway Kent Coast services in the company's early days. *IAL*

80
The inclined portals of the Shakespeare Cliff Tunnel, near Dover. *Charles Sergeant*

The Kent Coast trains had a string of resorts to serve between Ramsgate and Whitstable. Some had Dover portions detached at Faversham. The Dover line served Canterbury which in 1930 had a best time from London of 1hr 39min by the 10.44 Saturdays Only from Victoria, running to Faversham non-stop. On other days the best time was 1hr 50min by the 10.34 down. Although electrification to the Kent Coast had been among the Southern's plans before the war, it was not achieved until 1956 and so the former SECR timetables did not undergo the radical restructuring which took place on the LBSCR lines with electrification to Brighton, Eastbourne/Hastings, and to Portsmouth via the Mid-Sussex line (see Chapter 5). Some now almost forgotten travel possibilities existed over ex-LBSC routes, such as London to Brighton via Horsham and Shoreham; or via East Grinstead and Lewes; or London to Eastbourne via Eridge and Hailsham. There was also a through train from Chichester to London which took the Midhurst line to join the Mid-Sussex at Hardham Junction, then continued from Horsham via Dorking and Sutton. But these were journeys for the connoisseur of rural lines rather than the traveller in a hurry.

Some ex-LSW byways were operating in 1930 and few then doubted their future. There were four down trains and three up between Alton and Southampton Terminus via Alresford, joining or leaving the main line at Winchester Junction. The best time for the journey was 2hr 59min by the 4.15pm down. The Gosport branch had eight trains each way daily between there and Fareham. The Swanage branch saw through coaches from London, as well as having connections with the principal Weymouth trains at Wareham. More fortunate than these branches, Brockenhurst-Lymington has survived the cuts and still has a through train to and from Waterloo on Saturdays. In the summer of 1930 there were two down and three up Saturday through services, all of them restaurant car trains. Departures from Waterloo were at 9.40 and 11.38am; and from Lymington Pier at 11.12am and 1.32 and 4.01pm.

When thinking of the West of England service from Waterloo the mind tends to jump at once to Exeter and beyond. But the service to Salisbury should not be overlooked for in 1930 the city enjoyed three non-stop trains daily from London, and six on Saturdays, the journey times ranging between 1hr 50min and 1hr 30min. The departures at 10.24(SO), 10.40, 11.00 and 12.00 (Friday and Saturday only) were bracketed under the title 'Atlantic Coast Express'. Best time to Exeter at the beginning of the 1930s was 3hr 14min by the 10.40am but this had come down to 3hr 6min by the summer of 1939.

81
A Victoria-Eastbourne express near Southerham Junction, Lewes, is headed by 'U1' class 2-6-0 No 1907. *O. J. Morris*

The Waterloo main line working timetable in the 1930s was liberally provided with optional paths for boat trains, generally allowing about 1hr 40min for the journey to Southampton Dock Gates. Luxurious new Pullman cars were included in the trains from 1931. Boat portions might also be conveyed by the 8.26am and the 7.30pm Waterloo-Bournemouth trains, the coaches for the docks being detached at Eastleigh. All these workings were for ocean liner sailings, the liner being still a means of transport rather than a floating leisure centre (in fact it combined both functions). There was also the 9.00pm cross-Channel service from Waterloo connecting with the sailing from Southampton to Le Havre.

Until Grouping the LSWR and the LBSCR had competed for traffic to Portsmouth. Under the Southern Railway the principal services were concentrated at Waterloo in 1924, the Victoria trains being rescheduled as semi-fasts serving intermediate stations on the route via Horsham and Chichester. Waterloo introduced a regular-interval timetable of fast trains at 10 minutes to the hour for most of the day, with three down and four up non-stops making the journey in 1hr 38min. The Isle of Wight holiday traffic by train and boat was heavy in those days and holidays traditionally began on Saturdays. All trains from 9.50am to 1.50pm were non-stop on these occasions, with semi-fasts a few minutes earlier or later; and extra non-stops left Waterloo at 20min past the hour.

Although the LBSC route had lost its best trains from Victoria, many of the Saturday extras from Waterloo followed a 'hybrid' LSW/LBSC route in keeping with the recently integrated system. Leaving the LSW main line at Raynes Park, they travelled via Epsom and the Epsom and Leatherhead Joint line (LSW/LBSC), then to Dorking, Horsham and Portsmouth by the ex-LBSC route.

When the 'Schools' class 4-4-0s were allocated to Fratton for Portsmouth services in 1935, the Southern introduced a 90min non-stop schedule from Waterloo to Portsmouth & Southsea. In the July timetable of that year the 11.50am down was so timed, while the 1.50pm on Fridays and the 3.50pm were allowed 95min and 94min respectively with a stop at Fratton. In the Saturday timetable there were 11 trains between 7.50am and 3.50pm taking between 1hr 44min and 1hr 49min. The 10.20 and 11.25am and the 12.25 and 1.25pm were shown in the public timetables as non-stop to Portsmouth Harbour and labelled 'third class only'. At this time the Monday to Friday service to Portsmouth from Victoria or London Bridge showed eight through trains between 9.05am and 7.20pm with a best time of 2hr 22min by the 4.50pm from London Bridge. All were via Sutton and Dorking except the 9.05am which ran via Crawley. On Saturdays there were additional trains at 10.10 and 11.40am (via Dorking and Sutton) and at 1.32pm (via Crawley).

By 1935, however, the decision to electrify to Portsmouth was in the offing. The work was completed in 1937 and the Waterloo services reorganised. There were no dramatic changes in journey times but the hourly fast trains leaving Waterloo at 50min past the hours matched the timings of the best steam trains while calling at Guildford and Haslemere. On Saturdays extra fast trains left Waterloo at 15, 20 and 45min past the hour, all with intermediate stops and journey times between 95 and 97min. Throughout the week there were slow trains to Portsmouth at 27 and 57min past the hour. They carried an Alton portion which was detached at Woking. The 90min timing of the Waterloo-Portsmouth fast trains had not been improved by 1939.

Electric services to Brighton on the ex-LBSCR main line began on 1 January 1933. In the previous summer, the last of steam working, there were two fast trains an hour from Victoria to Brighton for most of the day from 9.05am to 11.05pm, departing generally at 5min and 35min past the hour. Non-stops making the journey in the hour left at 10.35 and 11.05am ('Southern Belle') and at 1.10, 3.05 ('Southern Belle'), 5.35, 6.05(SX), and 6.35pm. To these must be added the 5pm(SX) 'City Limited' from London Bridge. On Saturdays there were extra non-stops at 2.50 and 3.35pm, allowed 68 and 65min respectively. The last train down at night, 11.05pm, stopped only at Haywards Heath, to set down. Most trains included Pullman cars; on the 8.05pm down, calling at Horley, Three Bridges and Haywards Heath, they were described in the timetable as 'Pullman Supper Cars'. On Mondays to Fridays the 3.35pm (non-stop on Saturdays) called only at Haywards Heath. The 2.05pm(SO) and 4.35pm were also 'one-stop' trains, serving Preston Park and Three Bridges respectively. Others divided their stops between Clapham Junction, East Croydon, Horley, Three Bridges, Haywards Heath and Preston Park in various combinations. The 1.35pm on Saturdays was unusual among the faster trains in calling at Balcombe, probably for the benefit of ramblers. Trains making three or four intermediate stops took between 75min and 85min for the whole journey. Only the 12.05pm called at Redhill. The 11.35am(SX) detached a portion at Preston Park for Bognor via Hove and Worthing. Connections to Peacehaven by Southdown motor ombnibus were shown for all trains.

The electrification of the Brighton line included the Cliftonville curve from Preston Park to Hove and the coast line as far as West Worthing. Both Brighton and Worthing were therefore offered more frequent and generally faster services. Advertisements announced 'Six trains per hour all day — Comfort and frequency

82
A Saturday scene at Waterloo in the early 1930s. In the foreground Class U 2-6-0 No A611 heads the 12.40pm to Portsmouth; beyond it is the 12.40pm West of England train waiting to leave with 'D15' class 4-4-0 No E471 (on other weekdays a 'King Arthur' turn with a Salisbury engine). *G. J. Jefferson*

83
A boat train from Southampton Docks is hastened up to London by 'King Arthur' No 782 *Sir Brian*. *C. J. Grose*

84
A miscellany of Southern and Great Western rolling stock forms the Margate and Hastings to Birkenhead through train, with 'U' class 2-6-0 No 804 making smoke near Betchworth on the Redhill-Reading line. *Dr Ian C. Allen*

85
A Portsmouth express from Waterloo headed by 'King Arthur' No 781 *Sir Aglovale* joins the coast line from the 'Portsmouth Direct' at Havant. *Geoffrey J. Jefferson*

— You won't need a timetable'. The intending traveller to the Sussex Coast who had not looked up his train beforehand, indeed, would have had little to complain of. Departures from Victoria were as follows:

At the hour — non stop to Brighton in 60min (Pullman car)
25min past — East Croydon, Haywards Heath, Hove, Shoreham-by-Sea, Worthing, West Worthing (85min — Pullman car)
28min past — Clapham Junction, East Croydon, Redhill, Haywards Heath, Preston Park, Brighton (74min)
46min past — Clapham Junction, East Croydon, Purley and all stations to Brighton via Redhill (Reigate portion detached); (98min)

London Bridge had two departures an hour as below:

At the hour — New Cross Gate, East Croydon, Horley, Three Bridges, Haywards Heath, Preston Park, Brighton (74min)
16min past — New Cross Gate, East Croydon, Purley and all stations to Brighton via Redhill; Reigate portion detached at Redhill (74min)

There were corresponding up services, and the timetable in both directions was modified in the morning and evening rush hours. In the Victoria service three of the non-stop 1hr trains were all-Pullman.

Eastbourne and Hastings services were the next to be electrified. They tended to live in the shadow of those on the Brighton main line but by the time of the last steam summer timetable in 1934 they were providing a very adequate facility. On Mondays to Fridays there were 14 fast trains from Victoria between 9.40am and 11.40pm. The best time was by the 10.45am non-stop which reached Eastbourne in 1hr 20min. In this case the Hastings coaches travelled into Eastbourne and out again but on most services they were detached at Polegate, the usual pattern of stops being East Croydon, Haywards Heath, Lewes and Polegate. On Saturdays five extra trains terminated at Eastbourne with only one or two stops en route but, presumably because of weekend traffic conditions, were easily timed and were in fact little different from the daily trains with more stops. The best of these was the 6.45pm, calling at Lewes and Polegate and reaching Eastbourne in 1hr 31min. With the same stops, the 5.15pm took 1hr 33min, which allowed for detaching a through portion for Seaford at Lewes. Trains serving more intermediate stations took between 1hr 38min and 1hr 52min, this last schedule allowing for stops at East Croydon, Haywards Heath, Lewes, Polegate and Hampden Park.

Most trains stopped at principal stations between Polegate and Hastings but the 11.40pm only called at Bexhill and St Leonards Warrior Square. Hampden Park, on the outskirts of Eastbourne, was less well served by fast trains than Preston Park, its equivalent outside Brighton. Only the 12.03pm, 10.10pm and 11.40pm were scheduled to stop there, and for some reason lost in the mists of social history the 10.10pm only did so on Wednesday nights.

The electric service to Eastbourne, Hastings and Ore began on 7 July 1935. Departures from Victoria were now at 45min past the hour from 8.45am to 3.45pm. The next departure, at 4.35pm was the prelude to the business service but the departures at 45min past were resumed from 6.45pm to 9.45pm. Late night services were provided by an Eastbourne and Ore portion detached from the 10.25pm for West Worthing at Haywards Heath, and an Eastbourne portion detached at Haywards Heath from the 12 midnight train to Brighton, with a connection at Polegate for Bexhill, St Leonards and Hastings. Fastest time to Eastbourne was 1hr 20min by the 5.04pm from London Bridge which stopped only at Lewes, where a Seaford portion was detached. The 45min past the hour trains making the standard stops at East Croydon, Haywards Heath, Lewes, Eastbourne, Cooden Beach, Bexhill Central, St Leonards Warrior Square and Hastings took 1hr 24min to Eastbourne and 2hr to Ore. There were some grumbles at first because Hastings portions ran into Eastbourne and out again instead of being detached at Polegate.

The last of the Southern Railway's prewar electrifications to the coast was the Portsmouth No 2 scheme. This completed conversion of the former LBSCR routes to Portsmouth, including the section from West Worthing to Ford where the Mid-Sussex line from Horsham joined the coast line. The live rail was carried down the Littlehampton and Bognor branches, and westwards along the coast line to Havant where the existing Portsmouth No 1 electrification from Waterloo was joined. With the downgrading of their Portsmouth services, the LBSCR lines had been something of a backwater. Crawley New Town was as yet undreamed of. Steam trains ambled down the Arun valley, calling at pleasant country towns which still remained within their own boundaries and retained their personalities. Littlehampton and Bognor brought holiday traffic and a little commuting, but nothing on the scale of Brighton and the East Sussex resorts, and the Portsmouth trains provided the cathedral city of Chichester with its only through service to London. Indeed, the indignation of the Church had been aroused by the first cuts and decelerations when the fast Portsmouth trains were concentrated at Waterloo and its voice, among others, had been heeded when the next timetable was planned.

Electrification from 3 July 1938 brought a more consistent and regular train service. Fast trains to Portsmouth with a through portion for Bognor left Victoria at 18min past each hour from 8.18am to 4.18pm, and again from 7.18pm to 9.18pm, calling at principal stations and connecting at Arundel with a shuttle service to Littlehampton. Three trains in this sequence travelled via Three Bridges, the remainder via Sutton and Dorking. Journey times were 1hr 42min to Bognor and 2hr 12min to Portsmouth Harbour. Variations in the evening rush hour included two departures from London Bridge, one of them non-stop to Horsham via Three Bridges which reached Bognor in 1hr 35min. A similar business train from Victoria called only at Horsham and Arundel before taking up the usual pattern of stops, its Bognor Regis portion making the journey in 1hr 27min and the remainder of the train reaching Portsmouth Harbour in 1hr 56min.

As well as taking over the semi-moribund 'Thanet Limited' from the SECR, the Southern acquired two flourishing named trains from the LBSCR — the 'City Limited' and the 'Southern Belle'. The 'City Limited' was the older, its roots going back to the Brighton Railway's much criticised preferential treatment of first class passengers. Seeing Brighton as a place of residence for prosperous City gentlemen, the Brighton line provided them with a first class only service to London Bridge in the morning, and a similar return train at the end of the business day. The service remained first class only until 1919, although the 'Regulations to be observed by Passengers on the London Brighton and South Coast Railway' in the 1850s noted that 'By the Express Trains leaving Brighton at 8.45am and London at 5.00pm no Second Class carriages will be provided, except for Servants whose employers travel in the same train'.

Special stock had been built for the 'City Limited' in the later LBSC years, but in 1924 standard Southern Railway coaches were substituted, the formation consisting of 11 vehicles, one of which was a Pullman car. The total weight was about 360 tons. At that time the down train, 5.00pm from London Bridge, was running to Brighton non-stop in 60min, having reverted to a schedule first introduced in 1912 but decelerated during the war. The up train, 8.45am from Brighton, took 62min but from the summer of 1928 the service in both directions was in the level hour. In the last steam years the ex-LBSC Baltic tanks were regular power for the 'City Limited' and No 332 of that class worked the last steam-hauled service on 30 December 1932, running the 50.9 miles to Brighton in 57$\frac{3}{4}$min with a gross load of 385 tons. Electrification again brought new stock to the 'City Limited', similar to the other Brighton express sets but with a higher pro-

86
The down 'Southern Belle' Victoria-Brighton all-Pullman express near Coulsdon in the late 1920s. The locomotive is 'King Arthur' No 796 *Sir Dodinas le Savage*. *IAL*

portion of first class seating. The train was formed of two six-car units with a Pullman car in each. During World War 2 the Pullmans were withdrawn. In the few remaining years of the Southern Railway the trains made one or two additional stops with only a trifling addition to the journey time, and eventually these too were accommmodated within the 60min schedule.

The second named Brighton service was the 'Southern Belle', an all-Pullman train dating from 1908. It was, in fact, a service rather than a train for soon after its introduction it made two trips in each direction, later increased to three. At one period third class coaches were run with the Pullmans on the midday workings but the Southern Railway decided to make it an all-Pullman train again, with first class and third class Pullman cars only. The 60min non-stop schedule which had characterised the train from its inception was maintained, sometimes with loads at summer weekends of 11 or 12 Pullmans weighing about 400 tons. Ex-LBSC Baltic tanks coped well with this formidable task, but an allocation of 'King Arthur' class 4-6-0s brought welcome relief.

The last steam-hauled 'Southern Belle' ran on 31 December 1932, appropriately headed by the Brighton line's war memorial locomotive, 4-6-4T No 333, *Remembrance.*

The five-car Pullman units built to replace the steam-hauled cars were powered by the first Pullman electric motorcoaches in the world. Three services were run in each direction, usually formed of two units making a 10-car train. In 1934 the name was changed to 'Brighton Belle', which many thought was not a happy choice in a period when cheap steamer trips, similarly named, ran from seaside piers up and down the country. However, the Southern Railway had brought it upon itself by annexing the 'Belle' suffix for a Pullman train to Bournemouth. Both were 'Southern Belles' in one sense, and they had to be differentiated.

The 'Brighton Belle' was taken out of service at the beginning of World War 2 and the Pullman sets did not reappear until 1946. At first they ran with ordinary coaches, but by the end of the Southern Railway period the 'Belle' was an all-Pullman train again. It outlived the 'Bournemouth Belle' and the 'Devon Belle' — last of the Southern Railway's 'Belle' family — and by the time it was withdrawn on 30 April 1972 it was universally known simply as 'The Belle'. In 1908 the 'Southern Belle' had been hailed in LBSC publicity as 'the most luxurious train in the world'. It retained the afterglow of this glamorous image throughout its life although it had lost the drawing room furnishings of the early cars. Some were disposed to smile at an all-Pullman train for a journey of 51 miles. Perhaps it is best remembered as a train which allowed the traveller to the sea to step into a mobile hotel lounge at Victoria Station and be as unaware as he wished of the mundane circumstances of a railway journey. If the Brighton Railway had been able to build its terminus

87
No 21C11 *General Steam Navigation* at speed with the down 'Bournemouth Belle' at West Weybridge.
Wethersett Collection

88
'Lord Nelson' No 864 *Sir Martin Frobisher*, with large-diameter chimney, hauls a down Bournemouth and Weymouth express near Southampton.

as close to the sea front as had once been planned, the illusion would have been complete.

Many might have thought Bournemouth a more suitable destination for a Pullman service than Brighton, and the LSWR did in fact run first class 'Pullman Drawing Room Cars' in four Bournemouth trains in each direction but with the advent of restaurant cars they were withdrawn. The Southern Railway revived Pullman service to Bournemouth with the 'Bournemouth Belle' in 1931. At first it ran on Sundays only, making the journey non-stop, but in 1936 it became a daily service, a Southampton stop was added and a portion for Weymouth, previously operated was withdrawn. The down train, leaving Waterloo at 10.30am, reached Bournemouth Central in 2hr 6min. In the up direction departure from Bournemouth Central was at 4.45pm, and a fast run from Southampton Central to London brought it into Waterloo in a publicly-booked time of 2hr from Bournemouth (the working timetable allowed it a minute longer). The train ran to and from Bournemouth West.

After withdrawal during World War 2, the 'Bournemouth Belle' was reinstated in October 1946. Before

89
No 857 *Lord Howe* of the 'Lord Nelson' class, rebuilt with large taper boiler and round-topped firebox, passes Woking with a down semi-fast to Bournemouth.
Geoffrey J. Jefferson

90
'Schools' class 4-4-0 *Cheltenham* races through Hersham with an express for Bournemouth and Swanage. *Wethersett Collection*

the war it had been usually a 'Lord Nelson' duty; now the 'Merchant Navy' Pacifics, still streamlined, soon took charge. Timings at first were the same as in the 1930s but they had been eased by the time of nationalisation.

If the 'Bournemouth Belle' beguiled with visions of relaxation and comfort, the 'Bournemouth Limited' had a more businesslike sound. This was a two-hour non-stop Bournemouth-Waterloo service of ordinary stock put on in 1929, leaving Bournemouth at 8.40am and returning from Waterloo at 4.30. The train ran all the year round, but a second non-stop two-hour service for the summer months only was introduced in the same timetable, leaving Waterloo at 10.30am and returning at 5.15pm. The 'Limited' made a demonstration run on 4 July when the train of 13 coaches was drawn by No 860 *Lord Hawke*. It was reported that 'the finest running was done after New Milton, 85mph being attained between Hinton Admiral and Christchurch'. The train reached Bournemouth $1\frac{1}{4}$min ahead of schedule. Throughout the travelling was extremely smooth, as was 'particularly noticeable when the fastest running was being attained'. It was emphasised that the service would provide greater comfort for Bournemouth travellers by elimination of the Southampton stop. In 1930 the train was endowed with new coaches designed by Maunsell, 58ft long by 9ft wide, with centre-corridor saloons and end entry vestibules. They were in standard Southern green relieved with black and fine yellow lining. Lettering was in gold block letters, shaded black. In 1938 the 'Limited' stock was painted in Bulleid's malachite green livery and seven 'Schools' class locomotives were painted to match in the following summer. With the outbreak of war the train was withdrawn. Although primarily a Bournemouth service, its formation of some 11 bogies included sections for Swanage and Weymouth travellers.

The end of the Southern Railway was only months away when the first 'Devon Belle' left Waterloo on 20 June 1947. This was another all-Pullman venture and embarked on the hitherto not very lucrative enterprise of Pullman travel to the West Country. There had been little demand for the Great Western's 'Torquay Pullman' before the war. The 'Devon Belle' conveyed four cars for Plymouth and eight for Ilfracombe. The last car of the Ilfracombe portion was an observation vehicle rebuilt from earlier Pullman bodies, and furnished with swivelling armchairs and settees. A wide and virtually unobstructed view was afforded by the rear window which occupied the end wall from roof to waist level, and there were similarly deep panes on both sides, forming continuous walls of glass. The Southern route to the West was scenic on many stretches and the car enabled passengers to appreciate it.

Leaving Waterloo at noon, the first scheduled stop out of London was Sidmouth Junction. The train broke a long tradition by running through Salisbury without stopping but in fact pulled up at Wilton, the next station, to change engines. At Exeter, reached in 3hr 36min from Waterloo, the train divided. The Plymouth portion left first and after calling at Okehampton and Devonport ended its journey at 5.25pm. The Ilfracombe portion, with observation car, served Barnstaple, Braunton and Morthoe before

91
'N15X' class (Baltic tank rebuild) 4-6-0 No 2333 *Remembrance* runs under clear signals with an up Bournemouth express near Hersham. This engine carried the name of the LBSC war memorial engine, but others of the class were named after engineers. *C. R. L. Coles*

pulling into Ilfracombe at 17.33. The 'Devon Belle' began as a weekend service. After nationalisation it was increased to five days a week in summer, followed by further changes aimed at improving the economy of an operation which did not live up to expectations. A decline in patronage was accelerated by the proliferation of private cars on the roads, and at the end of the summer 1954 timetable the 'Devon Belle' was withdrawn.

Coming so close to nationalisation, the 'Devon Belle' had only tenuous roots in Southern Railway history. In contrast the 'Atlantic Coast Express' title dated back to the early Grouping years. An 11am departure from Waterloo for the West Country was traditional in LSWR days, when there were still thoughts of a competitive service to Plymouth. Southern Railway policy decided that Plymouth could be left to the Great Western as far as London traffic was concerned but that it was sensible to make a bid for Ilfracombe. There was an Ilfracombe portion on the 11.00 and around it the tradition of the 'Atlantic Coast Express' was built. The *Southern Railway Magazine* ran a competition with a prize of three guineas to find a name for the train. Four entrants suggested the same title of 'Atlantic Coast Express', inspired by the fact that Ilfracombe is on the Atlantic coast, as are the more westerly resorts of Bideford, Torrington, Bude and Padstow, all served by coaches on the 11.00. Guard F. Rowlandson of Waterloo submitted the first of the winning entries and won the three guineas. The runners-up received *King Arthur* locomotive paperweights.

Ifracombe was served from Paddington by a slip portion off the 'Cornish Riviera Limited' which was dropped at Taunton and proceeded by stopping train, reaching Barnstaple Junction 10 minutes after the Ilfracombe portion of the 11.00 from Waterloo. Here the two trains were combined for the final stage of the journey to Ilfracombe, but Southern passengers had enjoyed the advantage of a 30min later departure from London.

The 'Atlantic Coast Express' was noted for its number of through portions. When running as a single train outside the peak summer season it gave through service to more different destinations than any other British express. The first coach to be detached came off at Salisbury to serve stations onwards to Seaton. Coaches for Sidmouth and Exmouth were dropped at Sidmouth Junction. At Exeter the remainder of the train that was to go further was split into two sections: for Ilfracombe and Torrington (the Torrington coach proceeding separately from Barnstaple Junction); and for Plymouth, Padstow, and Bude (Padstow and Bude coaches coming off at Okehampton and splitting for their separate destinations at Halwill Junction). If the restaurant car section left at Exeter is counted, the train when it left London had conveyed nine separate portions.

In summer the 'Atlantic Coast Express' was

92
No 21C18 *Orient Line* heads the down 'Devon Belle' between Sidmouth Junction and Whimple.
Pursey C. Short

despatched from Waterloo in two parts on Mondays to Fridays, but on Saturdays at the height of the holiday season there were no fewer than eight departures bracketed under the same title. Locomotives were normally changed at Salisbury, 'Arthurs' or 'Nelsons' working to that point from London and 'Arthurs' (sometimes the smaller-wheeled 'S15s') taking charge between Salisbury and Exeter, although for a short time in 1930 a 'Nelson' shedded at Exmouth Junction worked through between London and Exeter. The train was allowed 1hr 30min from Waterloo to Salisbury. By 1939 the standard formation when not divided was 12 bogies. In the war years equivalent trains were run, but unnamed and slower. Sometimes loads were 16 or 18 coaches, which was too long for the Waterloo arrival platforms so that the train had to stop at Clapham Junction to be divided for the last few miles.

The name 'Atlantic Coast Express' reappeared in the 1946 timetables. By that time the Bulleid Pacifics were available but the London-Salisbury time was not restored to its prewar 90min and remained at 1hr 43min. The 83min booking from London to Salisbury

93
The 'Devon Belle' observation car. *BR*

which gave the Southern its first mile-a-minute schedule did not come until 1952, in the British Railways era. Subsequent accelerations took place in the shadow of inexorable rationalisation plans which were to transfer much of the Exeter main line to the Western Region and reduce the sections beyond Exeter to a 'withered arm'. Of the eight ultimate destinations of the 'Atlantic Coast Express' coaches, only Exmouth and Plymouth have passenger rail connections today.

The Southern Railway had connections with the Northern lines in the London area; with the Great Western via its Redhill-Reading branch and the GW Reading-Basingstoke branch; and with the LMS Bristol-Derby section via the Somerset & Dorset Joint line (joint LMS and Southern) from Broadstone Junction (near Poole) to Bath. Until 1930 the Somerset & Dorset had its own motive power but in that year the LMS took over the responsibility. At the same time the S&D blue livery was dropped, to be replaced by LMS colours for locomotives and Southern green for the coaches. Sunny South Sam had spread his message far and wide and all these routes carried important through services, with many relief trains and specials at summer weekends. The Basingstoke-Reading link also led via Banbury to the LNER (GC Section), providing a route to the Midlands, the North-East and Scotland.

Some of the through trains in the Southern Railway period dated from the pre-Grouping years. Two of them were named and probably for that reason are remembered long after their demise. The 'Pines Express' was first shown in the timetables with that name in 1927 but had actually begun as a Manchester and Liverpool to Bournemouth service in 1910. The route was by LNWR to Birmingham, then over the Midland cross-country main line to Mangotsfield and over the branch to Bath (Midland station). Here the train joined the Somerset & Dorset line and continued to join the LSWR proper at Broadstone Junction. Various changes occurred during the Grouping years. By 1939 the portion from Liverpool included a coach for Southampton Terminus which was detached at Cheltenham. A GWR train on what before Grouping had been the Midland & South-Western Junction Railway took it on via Swindon Town to Andover, and then over Southern Railway metals to Southampton.

Withdrawn in the war years, the 'Pines Express' was restored in 1946 and continued to run under British Railways until 1967, although reroutings after closure of the Somerset & Dorset line in 1966 diverted it from its traditional run over the former Midland North to West artery.

The second cross-country named train was the 'Sunny South Express', a joint venture of the LBSCR and the LNWR dating from 1904. Liverpool and Manchester were the starting points in the North;

94
A Lynton & Barnstaple mixed train leaves Barnstaple Town for Lynton with 2-6-2T No 761 *Taw*. Services on this narrow-gauge line were withdrawn on 20 September 1935. *Donovan H. E. Box*

95
'The long express from Waterloo that takes us down to Cornwall'. No doubt Sir John Betjeman had the 'Atlantic Coast Express' in mind and thought of it as in this picture of 'King Arthur' No 452 *Sir Meliagrance* heading westward with the train. *IAL*

Brighton and Eastbourne the destinations in the South. The route skirted London, leaving the LNWR main line at Willesden Junction to follow the West London and West London Extension Railways and join the LBSCR at Clapham Junction. In 1914 the service was suspended but it returned after World War 1 and continued through the Grouping period. At this time it was a weekend service for most of the year but ran daily in summer. The whole train ran into Brighton where another locomotive came on at the rear and took the Eastbourne and Hastings coaches on by the coast line. There were variations of this procedure at summer weekends when the Hastings portion might omit Brighton, travelling via Keymer Junction to Lewes. Through carriages were also run between Birmingham and the Kent Coast resorts, joining the ex-SECR main line out of Victoria at Factory Junction, Battersea; and a portion from Sheffield joined the 'Sunny South' at Northampton.

The north-south connections in the London area (Fig 8) were extensively used for freight traffic, and the complex of junctions near Battersea also provided for the interchange of wagons between the yards at Feltham, Norwood and Hither Green. The hump yard at Feltham was a Walker development begun during World War 1 to relieve Nine Elms depots and yard of sorting work. It was off the main Bournemouth/West of England line from Waterloo; trains from the west bound for Feltham diverged at West Weybridge, while traffic from the Central and Eastern Sections reached the yard over the 'Windsor lines' from Clapham Junction. The yard, precursor of many modern establishments of the kind in the years ahead, was also conveniently situated for access to the North & South West Junction line leading via junctions at Kew to the LNER (GC Section) at Neasden and the LMS (Midland) at Cricklewood. This line carried numerous through excursion trains at summer weekends but it had the inconvenience that those for the Central Section of the Southern were travelling towards London at Clapham Junction and had to make a circuit via Factory Junction, Herne Hill and Tulse Hill to join the Brighton main line at Streatham Common.

In spite of its policy of integrating the services of the various Sections, the Southern did not provide a direct connection between the Central and the Western Sections as they approached Clapham Junction. Victoria station was adjacent to the Imperial Airways terminal and a convenient starting point for trains to Southampton connecting with the Empire flying boat services in 1939. These specials in the down direction had to be routed via the Streatham junctions and Tooting to join the Western Section main line at Wimbledon.

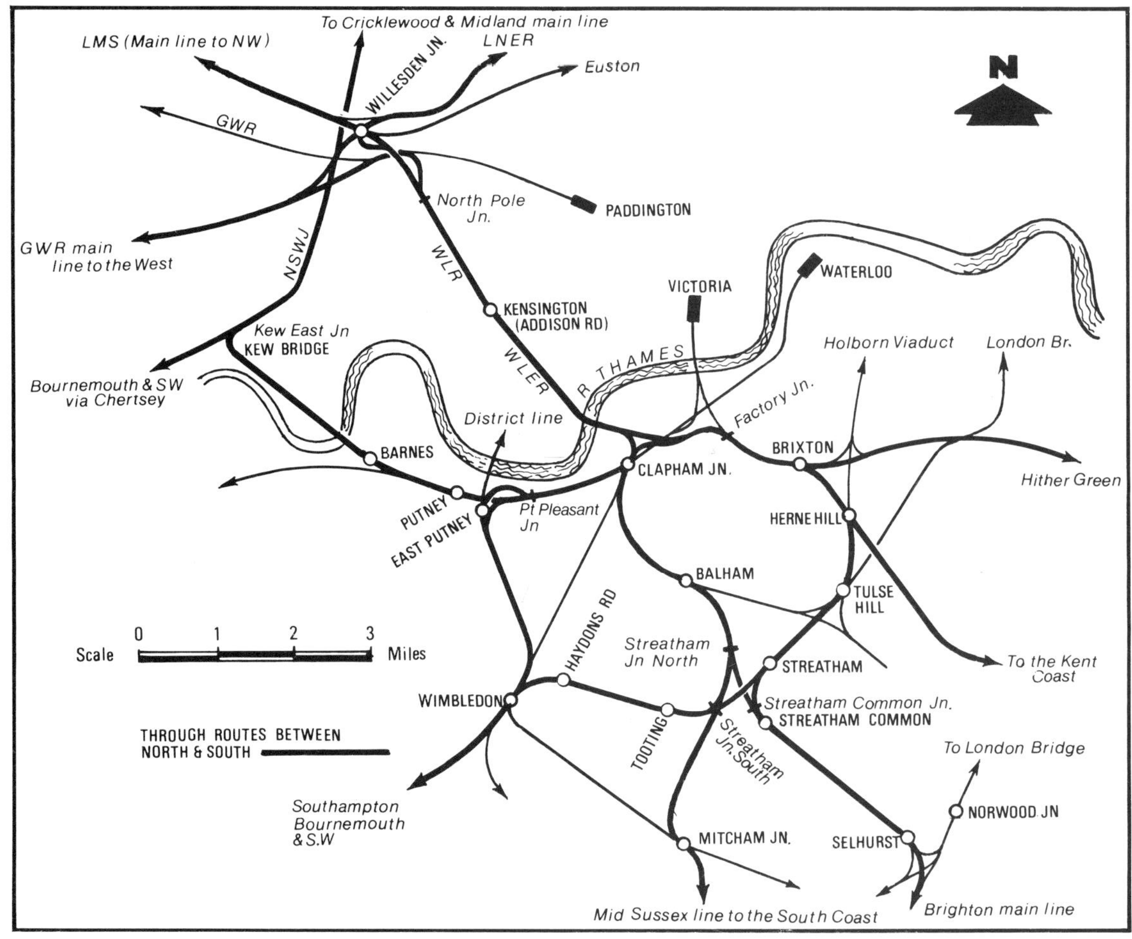

Fig 8
Connections between the Southern Railway and the Northern lines in the London area (through routes shown bold)

In the reverse direction the trains travelled from Wimbledon via East Putney, Point Pleasant Junction and Longhedge Junction to enter Victoria by the original low-level route.

At the time of Grouping all the principal resorts in the Isle of Wight were served by rail. Three companies had been involved. The Isle of Wight Railway and the Isle of Wight Central were merged with the London & South Western on the eve of Grouping; the Freshwater, Yarmouth & Newport came into the new Group shortly afterwards. Their equipment was by no means in line with the traffic potential of this popular holiday area and the Southern management was soon providing replacement motive power and coaching stock from the mainland. Klapper in *Sir Herbert Walker's Southern Railway* (see bibliography) tells much of this period of improvement and of the railway's debt to the energetic and resourceful A. B. Macleod who became responsible for motive power, rolling stock and commercial affairs in the Island. Exploiting the connections between the previously independent companies' lines, a named train, the 'Tourist', appeared in the 1930s running between Sandown and Freshwater via Newport, and other services labelled 'East and West Through Train' followed the same route or ran between Ryde and Freshwater.

Between 1924 and 1937 the Southern placed seven new ships in service between Portsmouth and Ryde. The Lymington-Yarmouth route received a new passenger ship in 1927 and a car ferry in 1938. A new ferry service for the motorist was opened between Portsmouth and Fishbourne in 1928 with roll on/roll off vessels.

96
IOW No 33 *Bembridge* leaves Yarmouth with a train from Newport to Freshwater. *Frank F. Moss*

97
Class H15 4-6-0 No 840 pulls away from Willesden Yard with a freight for the Southern and will soon join the former North & South Western Junction line to Kew at Old Oak Junction. These tracks are seen on the right.
C. R. L. Coles

98
Maunsell 'Q' class 0-6-0 No 540 passes Oxted with a short freight. *Wethersett Collection*

99
Victoria station, London, became the departure point for all regular 'short sea route' Continental services after formation of the Southern Railway

8 To the Continent

Connections between the former SECR and LCDR routes to Dover had been put in near Bickley by the SECR early in the century as shown in Fig 1, Chapter 1. The Southern Railway at once concentrated its Continental traffic at Victoria and in the autumn of 1923 announced services by the Short Sea Route at 9.05 and 11.00am, and 2.00 and 4.30pm. The former night service via Dover was withdrawn but the one via Newhaven-Dieppe continued. Best time to Paris was 6hr 55min by the 4.30pm train, which was a restoration of an earlier service. Dover Marine station had been built by the SECR with far-sighted provision for future development. The old LCDR Pier station would have been woefully inadequate for dealing with growing boat train traffic. Under the Southern Railway a programme of strengthening bridges was carried out so that the larger and more powerful locomotives coming into service could work over all the boat train routes. By 1925 'King Arthurs' were allowed on the main line to Dover and Folkestone via Tonbridge and Ashford. A year later the 'by-pass' to Ashford via Swanley and Maidstone was available to them, as well as the LBSC route to Newhaven Harbour. Bridge strengthening on the LCDR route to Dover via Chatham was completed by the summer of 1927.

The 'classic' Southern Railway boat train was the 'Golden Arrow'. It began in 1929 as a first class only all-Pullman service leaving Victoria at 11am, connecting at Dover with a sailing by a specially-built

100
'West Country' Pacific No 21C138 (later named *Lynton* and BR No 34038) passes Sydenham Hill on an up Continental express

101
'Lord Nelson' No 858 *Lord Duncan* leads the down 'Golden Arrow' in its all-Pullman days. *Real Photos*

steamer *Canterbury*. At Calais the 11-coach Pullman *Flèche d'Or* was waiting and brought passengers into Paris Nord at 5.35pm. This luxury service was soon overtaken by the depression years in the 1930s and its patronage was further diminished by competition from airlines. Ordinary first and second class coaches were soon included in the British train. A typical formation shortly before World War 2 was four Pullmans, six corridor coaches, and two six-wheel vans. At this period the return service was via Folkestone and the 'Arrow' was urged up the 1 in 30 from Folkestone Harbour to the sidings at Folkestone Junction, where a main line locomotive was waiting, by the exertions of two or even three 0-6-0 tank engines.

After wartime withdrawal, the 'Golden Arrow' was restored as an all-Pullman train on 15 April 1946. Reaction from wartime austerity made it popular with the more leisured travellers for a time but support for an all-Pullman train diminished in proportion with the growing appeal of air travel. Ordinary stock returned to the train, keeping it alive through nationalisation and into the era of electrification to the Kent Coast. In its final years it was hauled by an electric locomotive. The last 'Golden Arrow' journeys were at the end of the 1972 summer service.

A more original riposte to airline competition was the 'Night Ferry' through sleeping car train between London and Paris. The service required the construction of special train ferry terminals at Dover and Dunkerque, three ferry ships, and shortened versions of the International Sleeping Car Company's *wagons-lits* built to the British loading gauge. Services began on 14 October 1936. It was an exceptionally heavy train since a restaurant/kitchen set and ordinary coaches for passengers without sleeping car berths were included in the formation between London and Dover in each direction. At Dover and Dunkerque the sleeping cars were shackled to the deck with chains and although the shunting of the cars on and off the ships was accomplished in an unearthly and uncharacteristic silence it was accompanied at intervals by a clanking as of a hundred spectres shaking the gyves on their skeletal wrists. The sounds are no more than a softened and sentimental memory. After the war the train was restored and in the winter months was well patronised by businessmen. At breakfast between Dunkerque and Paris the man of affairs who habitually boasted to his colleagues that he always flew on his trips abroad could be seen hiding behind his newspaper to avoid recognition and facetious comments that aircraft diversions had taught him com-

102
Wagons-Lits cars loaded on to a ferry vessel at Dover for the crossing to Dunkerque. *BR*

103
Passengers with time for a more leisurely Channel crossing could travel from Waterloo via Southampton and Le Havre. The *Dinard* went into service in 1924. *Charles E. Brown*

104
The *Canterbury*, built specially for the Channel crossing on the 'Golden Arrow' service.

105
The *Worthing* was added to the ships on the Newhaven-Dieppe route in 1928.

monsense. But navigational and blind landing aids soon eroded this advantage of the 'Night Ferry'. After months of rumour and indecision the train left London for the last time on 31 October 1980.

Shipping services from Southampton to the Channel Islands, Le Havre and St Malo had been begun by a subsidiary of the LSWR formed in 1845. The Channel Islands ships competed with a service from Weymouth which was taken over by the Great Western Railway in 1888, but in 1899 the Channel Islands traffic was pooled between the two railways. The cross-Channel services from Southampton were continued and further developed by the Southern Railway which in 1924 put two larger vessels, the *Dinard* and the *St Briac* on the route to St Malo, and in 1930/31 equipped the Channel Islands service with three new ships.

On its formation the Southern Railway took over a fleet of 21 cross-Channel ships from the constituent companies together with 25 smaller vessels. Steps were soon taken to modernise the fleet, and in 1925 the *Isle of Thanet* and *Maid of Kent*, both of about 2,700 tons entered service on the Short Sea Routes. They were joined in 1929 by the *Canterbury* (2,910 tons), built as a first class only ship specially for the 'Golden Arrow' service. The *Canterbury* boasted a 'promenade' deck, the davits carrying the lifeboats being of a type which left the usual boat deck free of obstructions and available for 'promenading' in fine weather.

The Newhaven/Dieppe service was improved by the *Worthing* (2,294 tons) in 1928 and in 1933 the slightly larger *Brighton* (the fifth vessel of that name) joined the fleet, with accommodation for 1,450 passengers compared with *Worthing's* 1,288. Both ships had a top speed of 25 knots to reduce the time on the relatively long Newhaven/Dieppe crossing — 64 nautical miles compared with 21 from Dover to Calais and 28 from Folkestone to Boulogne.

In 1931 the Southern Railway put the special-purpose *Autocarrier* in service for travellers taking their cars across the Channel. The cars were still slung on board by cranes and manhandled to their parking positions by the crew. A daily service was provided between Dover and Calais (Paul Devot Quay) from 31 March, the passage taking 1hr 45min. Passengers with cars paid 10s (50p) single fare and the rates for cars varied from £1 17s 6d (£1.88) to £5 according to wheelbase. The boat deck was equipped in 'a comfortable and commodious manner so that travellers may enjoy the amenities to which they are accustomed when using the short sea route'. As for the cars, of which 35 could be carried, all under cover, it was rather quaintly claimed at the inaugural ceremony that they would 'no longer travel like mere luggage; also they would be accompanied by those who cared for them'. The ship could take 120 passengers.

The innovation of the Southern Railway period was the building of the three train ferry ships for the 'Night Ferry' London-Paris through sleeping car service. The *Twickenham Ferry*, *Hampton Ferry* and *Shepperton Ferry*, all named after crossings of the Thames, were vessels of 2,389 tons and could each carry 12 sleeping cars on four tracks. They were loaded 'roll on/roll off' at the stern, and the same procedure was used for motorcars, which were parked on garage decks with space for 25 to 30 vehicles.

Southern Railway ships did notable service in World War 2 and sustained serious losses. The last of the fleet, the *Invicta* of 4,178 tons for the 'Golden

106
The train ferry ship *Hampton Ferry* for the 'Night Ferry' through London-Paris sleeping car service. *BR*

Arrow' service went on wartime duties almost as soon as she was ready for traffic in 1939.

Arrangements for transfer between train and ship are an important factor in promoting passenger comfort. Folkestone was less convenient in this respect than Dover. Short platforms sometimes caused delays and passengers were in the open for some distance while walking to or from the quayside. The situation was improved in 1938 by increasing the length of Platform 1 at the Harbour station from 308ft to 700ft, providing a covered footbridge and additional roofing, and modernising the station buildings and refreshment rooms.

The SR general timetable gave brief details of Continental services, but their full ramifications had to be sought in the *Continental Handbook*. This was a publication in which the romance and the bald details of foreign travel rubbed shoulders. The Index to Stations was headed by two appropriate quotations from Shakespeare. *Henry VI*, Part 1, Act 5, Scene 1 contributed:

See them guarded and safely brought to Dover;
Where, inshipped, commit them to the fortune of the
 sea.

Having thus disposed of Dover-Calais, the Editor hit upon a lucky reference to Southampton in the prologue to *Henry V*, Act 2, with the Chorus promising:

The King is set from London; and the scene
Is now transported, gentles, to Southampton . . .
And thence to France shall we convey you safe,
And bring you back, charming the narrow seas
To give you gentle pass, for, if we may,
We'll not offend one stomach . . .

Continental main lines were shown on a folding map, with the suggestion that readers might like to consult the 'Itineraries of Famous International Expresses' printed on the back and trace their routes. Imagination could also wander further afield in contemplating the timetable headed 'London-China-Japan' by the Trans-Siberian Railway'.

Travellers to all parts started their journeys from Victoria, many of them by the services to Calais and Boulogne. The London-Paris table in the summer of 1930 was headlined 'London-Paris in 6hr 35min', referring to the 11.00am 'Golden Arrow' all-Pullman service. Among the numerous connections on the other side of the Channel was the 'Calais-Brussels Pullman Limited', arriving Brussels at 5.43pm. Passengers for Calais and beyond with first and second class tickets could travel by the 11.15am from Victoria (7hr 8min to Paris) or by the 2.00pm (6hr 55min). The 9.00pm from Waterloo provided a leisurely overnight service via Southampton-Le Havre, arriving in Paris at 10.15am.

Travellers via Dieppe wishing to enjoy '1C1 lux' appointments similar to those of the 'Golden Arrow' could travel in the Pullman on the 10.00am to Newhaven. The connecting train from Dieppe to Paris also included Pullmans at this time. Paris arrival was at 5.58pm. An earlier service at 8.30am from Victoria brought the traveller to Paris at 5.10pm. Overnight travellers leaving Victoria at 8.20pm reached Paris at 5.23am but passengers could remain in their carriages until 7.30.

The Newhaven-Dieppe route was primarily for Paris but its wider possibilities were stressed in a timetable note which read:

'The *night mail service*, 1st, 2nd and 3rd class (London dep 8.20pm) is specially recommended to businessmen as it enables a full day's work to be done in Paris. Further, its arrival at Paris (St Lazare) at 5.23am renders it possible to make connections with the early morning trains from Paris (Est), PLM, Quai d'Orsay, etc to all parts of the Continent'.

There was a similar note regarding the day service at 10.00am, which gave time to join the night expresses from the Paris termini. The Dieppe-Paris train on this service, leaving Dieppe at 3.24pm, included through coaches to the Gare de Lyon which arrived at 7.40pm, allowing passengers to the South to continue their journeys without change of station. Connection with the 7.55pm to St Gervais was shown in the table, but with the note 'not guaranteed', presumably in case of delays in negotiating the intricacies of the Ceinture. There was more margin for joining a train to Geneva and this connection was scheduled without qualification.

In 1930 the Batavier Line service from Gravesend to Rotterdam (Boompjes) was still in operation. A connecting train left Victoria at 6.10pm, called at Bromley South, and reached Gravesend Pier via the Gravesend West Street branch at 7.02pm. The steamer was timed to sail ten minutes later and to arrive at Rotterdam about 8 o'clock the next morning. There was no rail connection at the quay but the principal Rotterdam stations were about ten minutes away by tram or taxi. On the inward journey passengers could leave their luggage on board the ship at Gravesend and collect it later when it berthed in London.

The Southern's *Continental Handbook* was a book to be read as well as consulted. It waxed eloquent over the amenities and other features of the railway's fleet, and for further reassurance of the Briton venturing abroad published a two-page spread of portraits of the company's interpreters, who were stationed at Paris Nord and St Lazare, Brussels, Basle, Cologne and Le Havre.

9 Road and Air

The Transport Acts of 1928 gave the railway companies powers to engage in road transport of freight (as distinct from local collection and delivery services). In conjunction with the other three Groups the Southern participated in the purchase of Carter Paterson and Co Ltd and Hays Wharf Cartage Co Ltd (which included Pickfords). Sir Herbert Walker was a Director of Pickfords and in his day a new road parcels depot was built at Willow Walk, where the LBSC had had its London goods depot adjacent to the SECR Bricklayers Arms depot. In 1934 the two were merged under the latter name, but the name of Willow Walk was retained for the new road parcels establishment.

The Southern's own cartage fleet expanded from 278 to 757 vehicles over the decade 1929 to 1939 as shown below:

		1929	*1934*	*1939*
Motors	5-6 ton	115	172	68
	3 ton	—	—	14
	2 ton	157	261	161
	30cwt	2	6	56
	20cwt	2	—	23
	10cwt	—	—	19
Articulated	6 ton	—	—	41
Mechanical	6 ton	—	—	105
horses	3 ton	—	—	255
	2 ton	—	6	1
Tractors	10 ton haulage capacity	2	5	4
	15 ton haulage capacity	—	—	7
Horseboxes		—	3	3
Totals		278	453	757

The above fleet was employed mainly on collection and delivery work with an average daily mileage per motor vehicle of 25 miles. In 1938 the Southern was the only Group to show a profit on its own road haulage activities, gross receipts of £534,350 producing a surplus of £13,614. In 1939 some 600 horses were still employed but this was a decrease of 690 over the decade.

Participation in road passenger transport was by working agreements with a number of undertakings, in all of which the Southern held shares not exceeding one half of the share capital. The companies concerned were:

Aldershot & District Traction Co Ltd
East Kent Road Car Co Ltd
Hants and Dorset Motor Services Ltd
Maidstone and District Motor Services Ltd
Southdown Motor Services Ltd
Devon General Omnibus and Touring Co Ltd
Southern National Omnibus Co Ltd
Southern Vectis Omnibus Co Ltd
Thames Valley Traction Co Ltd
Wilts and Dorset Motor Services Ltd

A surprising advertisement in the Southern Railway timetable for July 1937 read: 'RAS. The Flying "Tip" of the Season. Brighton-Isle of Wight by multi-engined air liners of Railway Air Services. 15s day excursion. 4 daily services with rail connections'. The timetable showed that one service continued from Ryde to Southampton, Bristol (Whitchurch), Gloucester (Staverton, on request), Birmingham and Liverpool.

Railway Air Services Ltd (RAS) was incorporated on 21 March 1934, its board having one Director from each railway Group. The railways had been granted powers to operate air services in 1929, and by the time RAS was formed the Southern had already entered into an agreement with Spartan Airlines for providing a service between London and Cowes, which began on 1 May 1934. Spartan had been operating in the previous year but flying from London (Heston). Under the new arrangements the London terminus was transferred to Croydon. The Southern took a 50% share in receipts and expenses. On 12 December 1934 the Southern and the Great Western made an investment in Channel Islands Airways Ltd, a holding company formed to expand the operation of an airline which had been running a service to Jersey since the preceding year. The same two railways joined under RAS auspices in launching a service between Birmingham, Bristol, Southampton and Cowes on 30 July 1934, forming a close airborne parallel to the facilities offered by the Midland & South Western Junction Railway. It was extended from Birmingham to Liverpool, and from Southampton to Portsmouth and Shoreham in 1935. A year later Manchester and Gloucester (on request) were served, and the southern end of the route was extended to Ryde.

The SR/Spartan service changed its London terminal to Heston in 1935, and to Gatwick Airport in 1936. Gatwick, then on the opposite side of the A23 London-Brighton road to the present airport, was served by the station formerly known as Tinsley Green, then as Tinsley Green (for Gatwick Airport), and from 1 June 1936 as Gatwick Airport. There was a subway connection with the circular airport building, still in existence today and known as 'the beehive'. The present Gatwick Airport station is on the site of the former station for Gatwick racecourse, and traces of the former bearer of the name are now barely visible.

The first airport station, however, was Shoreham Airport. It had had an undistinguished beginning as Bungalow Town Halt and was closed when the Brighton-Worthing line was electrified. Railway Air Services activities brought it back to life; it was reopened as Shoreham Airport on 1 July 1935, but closed on 15 July 1940.

The Southern lost money in its association with Spartan Airlines and the London-Isle of Wight service was withdrawn in September 1936. An independent operator, Portsmouth, Southsea & Isle of Wight Aviation Ltd, was also flying to and from the Island, and from 1937 it operated a Portsmouth-Isle of Wight service connecting with the new electric train services of that year. This company's aircraft also flew to and from Shoreham Airport. Its operations tended to be informal as this personal reminiscence shows. I remember sheltering with a solitary fellow passenger in a kind of toolshed that did duty as a waiting room at the Isle of Wight airfield. It was a particularly atrocious day with pouring rain, and no sign of the scheduled aircraft. Soon, however, the putter-putter-putter of a taxying Puss Moth was heard and the machine came bouncing uncertainly into view out of a dip in the grass airfield. The pilot had been despatched from Portsmouth specially to pick up two intrepid travellers and fulfil the promise of the company's timetable.

Shortly after take-off the pilot turned to ask if either of us knew where Shoreham Airport was, as this was not his normal beat. Luckily we did, and when Worthing front came into view — deserted, rain-swept but geometrically straight — we advised him to follow it and keep a lookout for Lancing College chapel. One

107
An articulated lorry capable of carrying a 6-ton load.
Thornycroft Co Ltd

108
A Railway Air Services Ltd De Havilland Dragon as operating in May 1934. *British Rail*

heard much in those days of flying by *Bradshaw*; in 1920, indeed, the Air Ministry had asked the SECR to paint the names of Ashford, Tonbridge and Redhill on the station roofs to guide pilots flying between the Continent and Croydon. On this occasion, however, we preferred to fly by the *AA Book* and the method worked. With Lancing chapel in sight it was soon possible to spot the Shoreham control tower, and after two low passes to frighten sheep off the grass airfield a satisfactory landing was made.

The Southern's financial association with Channel Islands Airways was more successful than the earlier Spartan agreement and in June 1939 both the railways concerned increased their shareholding. At that time flights to the Islands were being operated from London, Shoreham, Southampton and Exeter. Services were maintained until June 1940. In June 1943 the Southern and Great Western secured complete joint ownership of Channel Islands Airways. Flights to the Islands were resumed in 1946 and by that time the route could boast the prototype Bristol 170 ('Wayfarer') 32-seater aircraft.

Although the Southern and Great Western had sponsored Railway Air Services routes in the South and West they were not happy in being involved in other activities of the group that were making a loss and at the end of December 1938 withdrew, forming a separate company, Great Western & Southern Airlines, to take over these and other routes, including some to the Continent (Fig 9). After the war there was a possibility of the railways forming the nucleus of an air network serving both the British Isles and Europe but with a change of Government that prospect disappeared. The policy for the air as for the railways was nationalisation. British European Airways was formed on 1 August 1946 and all scheduled domestic services were taken over by that corporation on 1 April 1947.

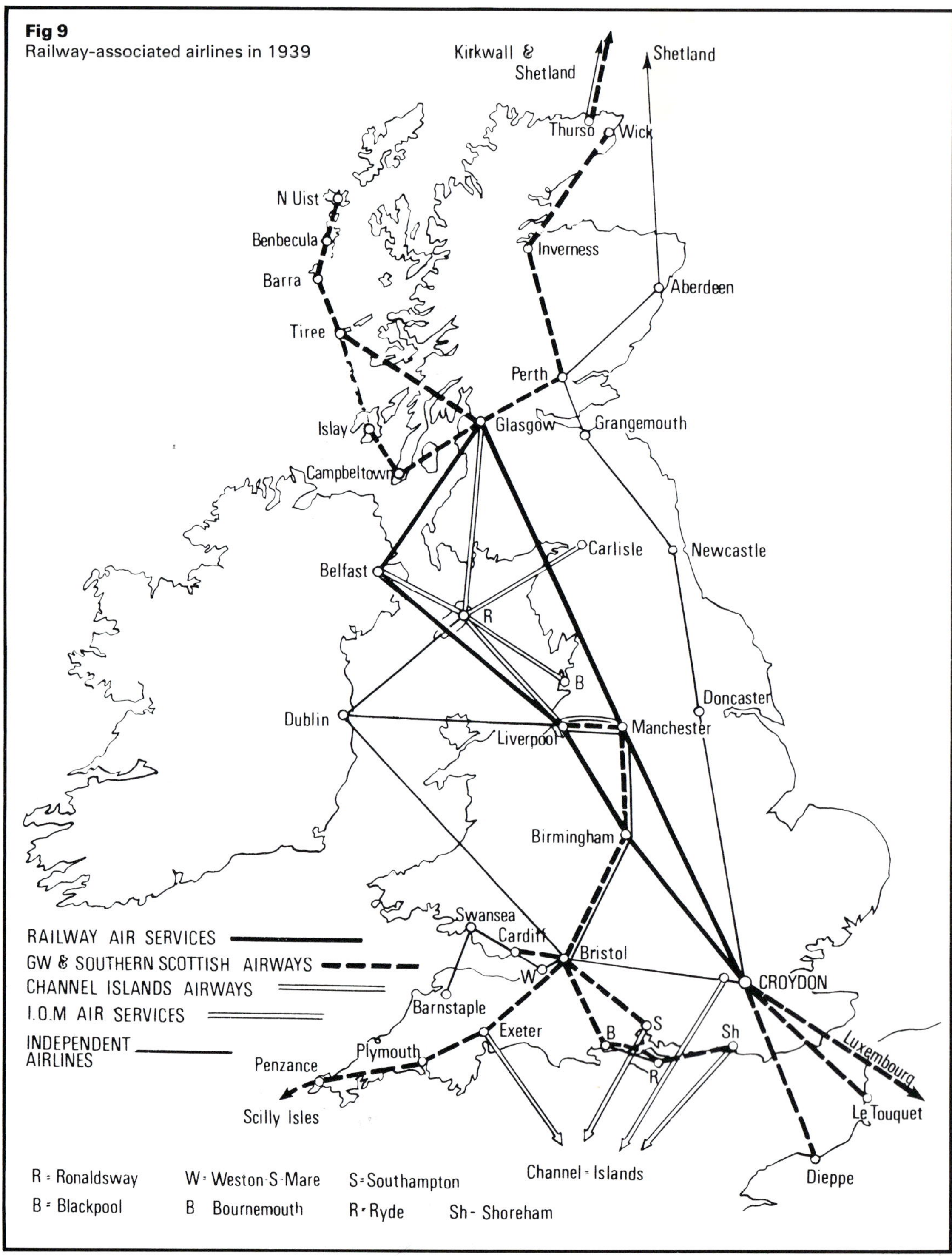
Fig 9
Railway-associated airlines in 1939
Kirkwall & Shetland
Shetland
Thurso
Wick
N Uist
Benbecula
Barra
Tiree
Inverness
Aberdeen
Perth
Islay
Glasgow
Grangemouth
Campbeltown
Carlisle
Newcastle
Belfast
R
B
Doncaster
Dublin
Liverpool
Manchester
Birmingham
Swansea
Cardiff
Bristol
W
CROYDON
Barnstaple
Exeter
S
B
Sh
Plymouth
Penzance
R
Luxembourg
Le Touquet
Scilly Isles
Channel - Islands
Dieppe
RAILWAY AIR SERVICES
GW & SOUTHERN SCOTTISH AIRWAYS
CHANNEL ISLANDS AIRWAYS
I.O.M AIR SERVICES
INDEPENDENT AIRLINES
R = Ronaldsway
B = Blackpool
W = Weston-S-Mare
B Bournemouth
S = Southampton
R = Ryde
Sh - Shoreham

Appendix 1 - Organisation

The headquarters organisation of the Southern Railway announced at Grouping comprised 15 departments as follows:

Executive
Secretarial
Legal
Accounting
Estate
Railway operating
Commercial
Civil engineering
Locomotive, Carriage & Wagon construction and maintenance
Docks and Marine
Electrical Engineering
Purchasing and supervision of horses
Purchase of stores and storekeeping
Medical
Police

At the top of the hierarchy was the General Manager, assisted by an Assistant General Manager and one or more Assistants to the General Manager as might be necessary. An 'Assistant *to*' was by no means the same thing as a full-blown Assistant and failure to distinguish between the two categories by the press was a frequent source of irritation at the top.

The headquarters officers and their departmental assistants were:

Chief Operating Superintendent
- General Assistant
- Locomotive Running Assistant
- Assistant for Rules and Regulations
- Staff Assistant
- Assistant for Train Services

Chief Commercial Manager
- Outdoor Commercial Manager
- Two Assistants to Outdoor Commercial Manager
- Indoor Commercial Manager
  - Two Assistants to Indoor Commercial Manager
  - Seven Divisional Commercial Assistants
- Assistant for Continental Work
- Staff and Statistical Assistant

Chief Engineer
- Deputy Chief Engineer
- Chief Assistant for Parliamentary & General Purposes
- Permanent Way Assistant
- New Works Assistant
- Assistant for Bridge and Roof Construction

Chief Mechanical Engineer
- Carriage & Wagon Superintendent
- Works Managers as may be necessary

The railway was divided into six Operating Divisions, each with a Divisional and an Assistant Divisional Operating Superintendent. They did not coincide with the Western, Central and Eastern Sections, although the same names were used. The Divisions were:

London (East)
Covering the bulk of the London suburban lines of the LBSC and SECR to points beyond Dartford, Chiselhurst, Chelsfield, Selsdon Road and Coulsdon (HQ London Bridge).

London (West)
All LSW suburban lines together with main routes beyond to Southampton Docks, Portsmouth via Haslemere, Hayling Island branch and Isle of Wight lines (HQ Waterloo).

Eastern
Most of Kentish lines east of Dartford, Chiselhurst, and Chelsfield; main line from east of Tonbridge, and certain branches extending into Sussex (HQ Ashford, then Dover).

Southern
Greater part of late LBSC system south of suburban area except for Portsmouth District lines, while including Tunbridge Wells and Hastings section of late SECR (HQ Brighton station).

Central
All LSW lines west of Basingstoke, and Southampton Docks line, as far as Salisbury, and to Dorchester and Weymouth, together with Fareham group of lines

between Southampton and Portsmouth (HQ Southampton West).

Western
West of England main line west of Salisbury.

Later in 1923 it was announced that seven engineering districts would come into force as from 1 January 1924: London (East), London (West), Portsmouth, Southern, Eastern, Central and Western (HQ Exeter Queen Street).

Principal officers of the company from 1923 to 1947 were:

General Managers	
Sir Herbert Walker, KCB	1923
Gilbert S. Szlumper, CBE	1937
Sir Eustace Missenden	1939
John Elliot	Oct 1947
Chief Engineers	
A. W. Szlumper	1923
G. Ellson	1927
V. A. M. Robertson	1944
Chief Electrical Engineers	
H. Jones	1923
A. Raworth	1938
C. M. Cock	1945
Chief Mechanical Engineers	
R. E. L. Maunsell, CBE	1923
O. V. S. Bulleid, CBE	1937

Appendix 2 - Numbering and Names

On formation of the Southern Railway locomotive numbers were prefixed by a letter showing their company of origin, as follows:

LSWR E; LBSCR B; SECR A

The position of the letter in relation to the number as displayed on the locomotive was variable, either above the figures or preceding them. On front buffer beams the letter was on the left, taking the place of the usual 'No', and the numerals on the right. In 1931 the letters were dropped. Eastern Section engines then had 1000 added to their numbers, Central Section engines 2000, and Western Section engine numbers remained unchanged without the 'E' prefix. The letters indicated the works to which the engines were allocated for overhauls, A for Ashford, B for Brighton, and E for Eastleigh. Maunsell's Z class 0-8-0Ts were built at Ashford and took the 'A' prefix but they were later transferred to Eastleigh for maintenance and their numbers (950-995) were unchanged when the 'A' was dropped.

The Western Section labelled certain locomotive classes with a power classification, using the letters A to K in descending order. The letter was painted on the side of the framing near the front buffer beam and appeared on the following classes:

A — G16, H15, H16, 'Nelsons', N15, Q1, S15, V
B — Q, T14
C — 700
D — D15, L12
E — S11
F — K10, L11
G — 0395
H — T9
I — T3, X6
J — A12
K — All tank engines (except G16, H16)

Naming of locomotives was not an LSWR tradition but it flourished on the Western Section with the advent of the 'King Arthurs' and was continued until the end of the Southern Railway. Maunsell revived the practice in the last years of the SECR with *River Avon*, the first of the 'River' class 2-6-4Ts, more of which were built and named after Grouping. That stronghold of engine naming, the LBSCR, only named one of the Marsh Atlantics, No 39, which became *La France* in 1913 in honour of a French Presidential visit to this country, but both series of these engines were later named by the Southern Railway.

The named classes of Southern Railway locomotives are tabulated below. 'Merchant Navy', 'West Country' and 'Battle of Britain' locomotives are shown with the numbering given by O. V. S. Bulleid which indicated wheel arrangement as well as the individual number of the engine in its class. The symbols had the following meanings:

1st numeral	No of leading axles
2nd numeral	No of trailing axles
Letter	No of driving axles (C=3)
3rd numeral	Locomotive number

The system differed from the Continental practice (eg 2-C-1 for a Pacific) in that the number of leading and trailing axles was given *before* the letter in order to separate these numerals from the locomotive number.

'River' class 2-6-4T (Rebuilt as 2-6-0 tender engines, unnamed)

A790 *River Avon*
A791 *River Adur*
A792 *River Arun*
A793 *River Ouse*
A794 *River Rother*
A795 *River Medway*
A796 *River Stour*
A797 *River Mole*
A798 *River Wey*
A799 *River Test*
A800 *River Cray*
A801 *River Darenth*
A802 *River Cuckmere*
A803 *River Itchen*
A804 *River Tamar*
A805 *River Camel*
A806 *River Torridge*

109
The 0-4-0T *Ironside* was one of two locomotives taken over when the LSWR purchased Southampton Docks in 1892. It is seen here still in Southern livery at Guildford shed shortly after nationalisation. *D. J. Farrer*

A807 *River Axe*
A808 *River Char*
A809 *River Dart*
A890 *River Frome*

'King Arthur' class (N15)

448 *Sir Tristram*
449 *Sir Torre*
450 *Sir Kay*
451 *Sir Lamorak*
452 *Sir Meliagrance*
453 *King Arthur*
454 *Queen Guinevere*
455 *Sir Launcelot*
456 *Sir Galahad*
457 *Sir Bedivere*

736 *Excalibur*
737 *King Uther*
738 *King Pellinore*
739 *King Leodegrance*
740 *Merlin*
741 *Joyous Gard*
742 *Camelot*
743 *Lyonnesse*
744 *Maid of Astolat*
745 *Tintagel*
746 *Pendragon*
747 *Elaine*
748 *Vivien*
749 *Iseult*
750 *Morgan le Fay*
751 *Etarre*
752 *Linette*
753 *Melisande*
754 *The Green Knight*
755 *The Red Knight*

763 *Sir Bors de Ganis*
764 *Sir Gawain*
765 *Sir Gareth*
766 *Sir Geraint*
767 *Sir Valence*
768 *Sir Balin*
769 *Sir Balan*
770 *Sir Prianius*
771 *Sir Sagramore*
772 *Sir Percival*
773 *Sir Lavaine*
774 *Sir Gaheris*
775 *Sir Agravaine*
776 *Sir Galagars*
777 *Sir Lamiel*
778 *Sir Pelleas*
779 *Sir Colgrevance*
780 *Sir Persant*
781 *Sir Aglovale*
782 *Sir Brian*
783 *Sir Gillemere*
784 *Sir Nerovens*
785 *Sir Mador de la Porte*
786 *Sir Lionel*
787 *Sir Menadeuke*
788 *Sir Urre of the Mount*
789 *Sir Guy*
790 *Sir Villiars*
791 *Sir Uwaine*
792 *Sir Hervis de Revel*
793 *Sir Ontzlake*
794 *Sir Ector de Maris*
795 *Sir Dinadan*
796 *Sir Dodinas le Savage*
797 *Sir Blamor de Ganis*
798 *Sir Hectimere*
799 *Sir Ironside*
800 *Sir Meleaus de Lile*
801 *Sir Meliot de Logres*
802 *Sir Durnore*
803 *Sir Harry le Fise Lake*
804 *Sir Cador of Cornwall*
805 *Sir Constantine*
806 *Sir Galleron*

Note:
Nos 448-457 built at Eastleigh by the Southern Railway
Nos 736-755 were the Urie engines
Nos 763-792 built by North British
Nos 793-806 built by North British with six-wheel tenders

'Lord Nelson' class

850 *Lord Nelson*
851 *Sir Francis Drake*
852 *Sir Walter Raleigh*
853 *Sir Richard Grenville*
854 *Howard of Effingham*
855 *Robert Blake*
856 *Lord St Vincent*
857 *Lord Howe*
858 *Lord Duncan*
859 *Lord Hood*
860 *Lord Hawke*
861 *Lord Anson*
862 *Lord Collingwood*
863 *Lord Rodney*
864 *Sir Martin Frobisher*
865 *Sir John Hawkins*

'Schools' class (V)
900 *Eton*
901 *Winchester*
902 *Wellington*
903 *Charterhouse*
904 *Lancing*
905 *Tonbridge*
906 *Sherborne*
907 *Dulwich*
908 *Winchester*
909 *St Paul's*
910 *Merchant Taylors*
911 *Dover*
912 *Downside*
913 *Christ's Hospital*
914 *Eastbourne*
915 *Brighton*
916 *Whitgift*
917 *Ardingly*
918 *Hurstpierpoint*
919 *Harrow*
920 *Rugby*
921 *Shrewsbury*
922 *Marlborough*
923 *Bradfield*
924 *Haileybury*
925 *Cheltenham*
926 *Repton*
927 *Clifton*
928 *Stowe*
929 *Malvern*
930 *Radley*
931 *King's Wimbledon*
932 *Blundells*
933 *King's Canterbury*
934 *St Lawrence*
935 *Sevenoaks*
936 *Cranleigh*
937 *Epsom*
938 *St Olave's*
939 *Leatherhead*

'Remembrance' class (N15X)
2327 *Trevithick*
2328 *Hackworth*
2329 *Stephenson*
2330 *Cudworth*
2331 *Beattie*
2332 *Stroudley*
2333 *Remembrance*

Ex-LBSC Atlantics
'H1' class
2037 *Selsey Bill*
2038 *Portland Bill*
2039 *Hartland Point*
2040 *St Catherine's Point*
2041 *Peveril Point*
'H2' Class
2421 *South Foreland*
2422 *North Foreland*
2423 *The Needles*
2424 *Beachy Head*
2425 *Trevose Head*
2426 *St Alban's Head*

'Merchant Navy' class
21C1 *Channel Packet*
21C2 *Union Castle*
21C3 *Royal Mail*
21C4 *Cunard White Star*
21C5 *Canadian Pacific*
21C6 *Peninsular & Orient SN Co*
21C7 *Aberdeen (Commonwealth)*
21C8 *Shaw Savill*
21C9 *Orient Line*
21C10 *Blue Star*
21C11 *General Steam Navigation*
21C12 *United States Line*
21C13 *Blue Funnel*
21C14 *Nederlands Line*
21C15 *Rotterdam Lloyd*
21C16 *Elders & Fyffes*
21C17 *Belgian Marine*
21C18 *British India Line*
21C19 *French Line CGT*
21C20 *Bibby Line*
Note: Renumbered 35001-20 by BR and additional engines built; 35021-30

'West Country' class
21C101 *Exeter*
21C102 *Salisbury*
21C103 *Plymouth*
21C104 *Yeovil*
21C105 *Barnstaple*
21C106 *Bude*
21C107 *Wadebridge*
21C108 *Padstow*
21C109 *Lyme Regis*
21C110 *Sidmouth*
21C111 *Tavistock*
21C112 *Launceston*
21C113 *Okehampton*
21C114 *Budleigh Salterton*
21C115 *Exmouth*
21C116 *Bodmin*
21C117 *Ilfracombe*
21C118 *Axminster*
21C119 *Bideford*
21C120 *Seaton*

21C121 *Dartmoor*
21C122 *Exmoor*
21C123 *Blackmoor Vale*
21C124 *Tamar Valley*
21C125 *Whimple*
21C126 *Yes Tor*
21C127 *Taw Valley*
21C128 *Eddystone*
21C129 *Lundy*
21C130 *Watersmeet*
21C131 *Torrington*
21C132 *Camelford*
21C133 *Chard*
21C134 *Honiton*
21C135 *Shaftesbury*
21C136 *Westward Ho!*
21C137 *Clovelly*
21C138 *Lynton*
21C139 *Boscastle*
21C140 *Crewkerne*
21C141 *Wilton*
21C142 *Dorchester*
21C143 *Coombe Martin*
21C144 *Woolacombe*
21C145 *Ottery St Mary*
21C146 *Braunton*
21C147 *Callington*
21C148 *Crediton*

'Battle of Britain' class

21C149 *Anti-Aircraft Command*
21C150 *Royal Observer Corps*
21C151 *Winston Churchill*
21C152 *Lord Dowding*
21C153 *Sir Keith Park*
21C154 *Lord Beaverbrook*
21C155 *Fighter Pilot*
21C156 *Croydon*
21C157 *Biggin Hill*
21C158 *Sir Frederick Pile*
21C159 *Sir Archibald Sinclair*
21C160 *75 Squadron*
21C161 *73 Squadron*
21C162 *17 Squadron*
21C163 *299 Squadron*
21C164 *Fighter Command*
21C165 *Hurricane*
21C166 *Spitfire*
21C167 *Tangmere*
21C168 *Kenley*
21C169 *Hawkinge*
21C170 *Manston*

Note: 'West Country' and 'Battle of Britain' classes renumbered 34001-70 by BR and additional engines built; 34071-110

'B4' class (Dock Engines)*

81 *Jersey*
85 *Alderney*
86 *Havre*
89 *Trouville*
90 *Caen*
93 *St Malo*
95 *Honfleur*
96 *Normandy*
97 *Brittany*
98 *Cherbourg*
101 *Dinan*
102 *Granville*
147 *Dinard*
176 *Guernsey*

*0-4-0 side tanks designed by Adams and built 1891-3 at Nine Elms for shunting at docks, etc.

'0458' class**

734 *Clausentum*
3458 *Ironside*

**0-4-0T acquired 1892 on purchase of Southampton Docks.

Isle of Wight engines

'E1' Class

1 *Medina*
2 *Yarmouth*
3 *Ryde*
4 *Wroxall*

'A1X' Class

8 *Freshwater*
11 *Newport*
13 *Carisbrooke*

'O2' class

14 *Fishbourne*
15 *Cowes*
16 *Ventnor*
17 *Seaview*
18 *Ningwood*
19 *Osborne*
20 *Shanklin*
21 *Sandown*
22 *Brading*
23 *Totland*
24 *Calbourne*
25 *Godshill*
26 *Whitwell*
27 *Merstone*
28 *Ashey*
29 *Alverstone*
30 *Shorwell*
31 *Chale*
32 *Bonchurch*
33 *Bembridge*

Miscellaneous

756 *A. S. Harris* (0-6-0T)
757 *Earl of Mount Edgcumbe* (0-6-2T)
758 *Lord St Levan* (0-6-2T)
949 *Hecate* (0-8-0T)

Note: Nos 756-758 were taken over from the Plymouth, Devonport & South Western Junction Railway; No 949 was acquired from the Kent & East Sussex Railway.

Numbering of unnamed classes

Locomotives in the classes built by the Southern Railway which did not receive names were numbered as follows:

Class	*Wheel arrgt*	*Nos*
L1	4-4-0	753-759, 782-789
N	2-6-0	A823-875, 1400-1414
N1	2-6-0	A876-880
Q	0-6-0	530-549
Q1	0-6-0	C1-C40
S15	4-6-0	823-837
U	2-6-0	A610-639
U1	2-6-0	A891-900, 1901-1910
W	2-6-4T	1911-1915
Z	0-8-0T	950-957

HEADCODES

Southern Railway steam locomotive headcodes indicated route rather than class of train. They were modified in 1934 when trains working over 'foreign' metals carried a code corresponding to the standard express code, whether fast or slow. This did not apply, however, on the GW sections Exeter St Davids-Cowley Bridge Junction or Devonport-Laira. Southern trains proceeding into Devon or Cornwall from Exeter Central carried one of three codes according to whether their destinations were Ilfracombe, Plymouth or North Cornwall. The accompanying diagrams show the headcodes in use in the last years of the Southern Railway.

Constituents of the Southern Railway had used both letter and figure headcodes for electric trains. The Southern introduced new number codes for the Sutton and Coulsdon North services of 1925 but indicated South London line trains with the letters SL. As electrification proceeded, number codes were used exclusively.

Locomotive headcodes.

SOME S.R. LOCOMOTIVE HEAD SIGNALS

This list is not complete and gives only the principal one and two disc (or lamp) codes.

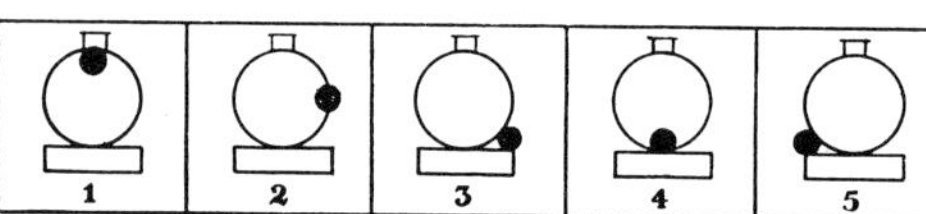

NO. 1

Victoria and Dover via Chatham
Loughborough Sidings to Holborn
Ashford and Hastings
Reading and Margate via Redhill
Eastleigh and Bulford via Chandlers Ford and Andover
Southampton Term. and Brockenhurst and Weymouth via Wimborne
Weymouth, Portland and Easton
Plymouth Friary and Tavistock
Woking and Reading via Virginia Water West Curve
Exeter Central and Ilfracombe
Bodmin and Wadebridge
Petersfield and Midhurst
Exeter Central and Exmouth

NO. 2

London Bridge or Bricklayers' Arms and Portsmouth via Quarry line and Horsham
Via Mid Kent line and Beckenham Junction
Ashford and Eastbourne direct
Waterloo or Nine Elms and Southampton Terminus, direct (not boat trains)
Willesden and Feltham Yard, via Gunnersbury
Waterloo or Nine Elms and Windsor, via Twickenham
Southampton Central to Lymington
Yeovil Junction and Yeovil Town
Seaton Junction and Seaton
Barnstaple Junction and Torrington
Halwill and Bude

NO. 3

London Bridge or Bricklayers' Arms and Brighton via Quarry line
Tonbridge and Brighton via Eridge
Hastings via Mid Kent line, Oxted, Crowhurst Junction and Tonbridge
Dunton Green and Westerham
Ashford and Margate, via Canterbury West
Lydd Branch
Canterbury West and Whitstable Harbour
Sandling Junction and Hythe
Folkestone Junction and Folkestone Harbour
Crowhurst and Bexhill
Swanley Junction and Gravesend West Street
Sittingbourne and Sheerness
Queenborough and Leysdown
Deal and Kearsney

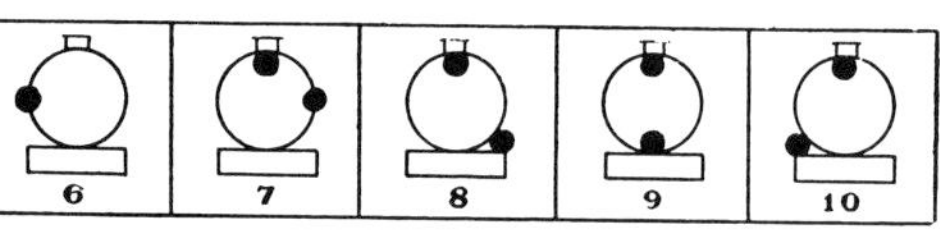

Gravesend Central and Allhallows on Sea or Port Victoria
All stations to Feltham (except via Mortlake)
Weymouth and Portland Easton (goods trains)
Bournemouth West and Brockenhurst, via Wimborne

NO. 4

Victoria or Battersea Yard and Brighton via Redhill
Oxted and Eastbourne via Eridge
London Bridge and New Cross Gate via Bricklayers' Arms Junction
Horsham and Brighton
Brookwood and Bisley Camp
Alton and Fareham
Bentley and Bordon
Salisbury and Bulford
Axminster and Lyme Regis
Tipton St. John's and Exmouth
Wareham and Swanage
Brockenhurst and Lymington Pier
Bere Alston and Callington

NO. 5

Oxted and Tunbridge Wells West via East Grinstead (H.L.)
Pulborough, Midhurst and Chichester
Havant and Hayling Island
London Bridge and Bricklayers' Arms
Tonbridge and Maidstone West
Ashford (Kent) and Dover via Minster and Deal
Elham Valley line
Stewarts Lane to Victoria
Southampton Docks and Nine Elms, via main line (market goods, fruit or potato train)
Light engines to Nine Elms

NO. 6

London Bridge or Bricklayers' Arms and Dover or Ramsgate via East Croydon, Oxted and Tonbridge
Tonbridge and Hawkhurst
Battersea Yard and Kensington
Waterloo or Nine Elms and Reading, via Twickenham
Willesden and Feltham Yard, via Kew East Junction
Exeter Central and Sidmouth
Plymouth Friary and Turnchapel
Eastleigh or Southampton and Fawley
Bournemouth Central and Brockenhurst, via Wimborne
Torrington and Halwill

NO. 7

Victoria or Battersea Yard and Portsmouth via Quarry line and Horsham
Via Maidstone East line to Victoria or Holborn
Waterloo or Nine Elms and Southampton Docks, via Brentford, Chertsey and Woking

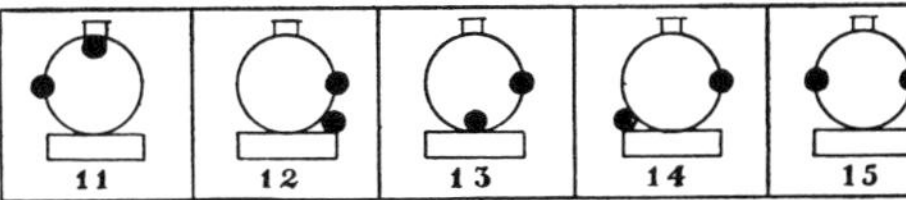

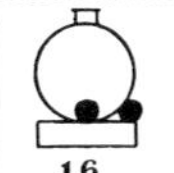

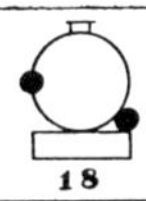

NO. 8

London Bridge or Bricklayers' Arms and Eastbourne or Hastings via Quarry line
Victoria or West London line and Ramsgate via Herne Hill or Catford loop
London Bridge or Bricklayers' Arms and Hastings via Chislehurst and Tunbridge Wells Central
West London line to East Croydon via Crystal Palace (L.L.)
Special boat trains Waterloo and Southampton Docks via Northam
Special boat trains from Southampton Docks to Waterloo via Millbrook
Southampton and Andover via Redbridge

NO. 9

Victoria or Battersea Yard and Eastbourne or Hastings via Quarry line
London and Hither Green Sidings
Victoria and Folkestone Harbour or Dover Marine via Swanley, Otford and Tonbridge
Waterloo or Nine Elms and Plymouth
Bournemouth Central and Dorchester goods trains
Battersea Yard and Brent, via New Kew Jct.
Southampton Terminus and Portsmouth Harbour, via Netley

NO. 10

London Bridge or Bricklayers' Arms and Portsmouth via Redhill and Horsham
Victoria or Battersea Yard and Norwood Yard via Crystal Palace (L.L.)
London Bridge and New Cross Gate to Eardley Sidings via Peckham Rye
Deptford Wharf and New Cross Gate
London Bridge or Bricklayers' Arms and Folkestone or Dover via Chislehurst, Tonbridge and Ashford
Dover and Margate via Deal and Minster loop
Special boat trains Waterloo to Southampton Docks via Milbrook

NO. 11

Victoria or Battersea Yard and Portsmouth via Redhill and Horsham
Via Dartford loop line
Victoria or Holborn and Hastings Branch via Orpington loop and Tunbridge Wells Central
Bricklayers' Arms and Guildford via Leatherhead and Effingham Jct.
Waterloo or Nine Elms and Southampton Terminus, via Alton
Salisbury and Bournemouth West, via Wimborne
Fareham and Gosport
Ballast trains to Meldon Quarry from Exeter Central and stations west thereof

NO. 12

Victoria or Battersea Yard and Portsmouth via Mitcham Junction
London Bridge or Bricklayers' Arms and Eastbourne or Hastings via Redhill
Victoria, Stewarts Lane or Holborn to North Kent line via Nunhead line
Nine Elms and Feltham Yard, via Mortlake
Exeter Central to Nine Elms (market goods and fish)
Down main line goods trains terminating at Woking

NO. 13

London Bridge or Bricklayers' Arms and Brighton via Redhill
Oxted and Brighton via East Grinstead (L.L.) and Lewes
Three Bridges and Tunbridge Wells West
West London line to Norwood Yard via Thornton Heath
Victoria or Holborn to Dover via Nunhead line and Maidstone East
Parcels and empty trains Waterloo to Clapham Junction (Kensington sidings)
Feltham Yard and Neasden, via Kew East Junction
Portsmouth Harbour or Portsmouth and Southsea to Fratton Loco. Depot
Exeter Central and Exmouth Junction
Bournemouth West to Dorchester
Southampton and Salisbury via Redbridge

NO. 14

London Bridge and Portsmouth via Mitcham Junction
London Bridge, Oxted and Tunbridge Wells West via Hever
Oxted and Lewes or Seaford or Eastbourne via Haywards Heath and Keymer Junction (change to No. 5 or No. 21 code at Lewes)
London Bridge or Bricklayers' Arms and Dover via Chislehurst loop and Maidstone East
Waterloo or Nine Elms and Brockenhurst and Bournemouth West, via Sway

NO. 15

Via Bexley Heath line
Victoria, Stewarts Lane or Holborn via Nunhead line and Bexley Heath
Oxted and Brighton via Haywards Heath
Waterloo or Nine Elms and Reading, via loop line
All trains terminating at Portsmouth and Southsea (trains from Salisbury to carry No. 17 to Eastleigh)
Exeter Central and Padstow
Light engines, Bournemouth Central or Bournemouth West to Bournemouth Central, via triangle to turn
Light engines Eastleigh Loco, to Portsmouth and Southsea
Light engines to Guildford Loco. via Woking (except via Staines)

NO. 16

London Bridge or Bricklayers' Arms and Portsmouth via West Croydon
Victoria or Battersea Yard and Eastbourne or Hastings via Redhill
Oxted and Brighton via Eridge
London Bridge or Bricklayers' Arms and Ramsgate via Tonbridge and Canterbury West
Waterloo or Nine Elms and Woking, via Richmond and Chertsey
Milk and empty trains to Clapham Junction, via Byfleet curve and Richmond

NO. 17

London Bridge or Bricklayers' Arms and Tonbridge or Reading via East Croydon and Redhill (also Tonbridge and Reading)
Brighton and Hove via Preston Park Spur
Three Bridges and Eridge
Victoria or Holborn and Folkstone or Dover via Orpington loop, Tonbridge and Ashford
London Bridge or Bricklayers' Arms and Gillingham, Faversham Ramsgate or Dover via Chislehurst loop and Chatham
Waterloo or Nine Elms and Clapham Junction (empty trains and light engines)
Passenger trains Bournemouth Central and Weymouth

NO. 18

London Bridge or Bricklayers' Arms and Dover, Ramsgate or Hastings via Chislehurst, Swanley, Otford and Sevenoaks
Victoria, Oxted and Tunbridge Wells West via Hever
Holborn and Ramsgate via Herne Hill or Catford loop
Light engines, and trains requiring to run to up main loop Clapham Junction, from stations westward
Southampton and Andover, via Eastleigh
Light engines or engines with vehicles attached running round the triangle at Bournemouth West to turn

NO. 19

Victoria or Battersea Yard and Brighton via Quarry line
London Bridge or New Cross Gate and Norwood Yard
Tunbridge Wells West and Eastbourne
Victoria or Holborn and Ramsgate, Dover or Hastings via Nunhead line and Tonbridge
Horsham and Guildford
Waterloo or Nine Elms and Southampton Docks via East Putney
Salisbury and Portsmouth Harbour, via Eastleigh
Portsmouth and Southsea to Salisbury, via Eastleigh

NO. 20

Victoria, Stewarts Lane or Holborn to Ramsgate via Nunhead line, Chislehurst and Chatham
London Bridge or Bricklayers' Arms and North Kent line via Greenwich
Via Streatham Spur
Feltham Yard and Brent, via Kew East Junction
Clapham Junction and Kensington
Portsmouth and Southsea to Salisbury, via Redbridge

NO. 21

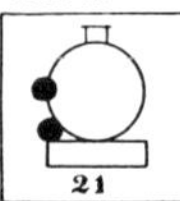

Victoria and Newhaven Harbour
Victoria or Holborn to Ramsgate via Nunhead line and Maidstone East
Waterloo or Nine Elms and Portsmouth, via Woking and Guildford
Light engines from all stations to Feltham Loco.
Light engines from all stations West of Basingstoke to Eastleigh Loco.

There are several three disc codes in use though most of these are for race specials. The Plymouth-Brighton through service is denoted by a three disc code and Royal Specials utilise the standard British four lamp head signal.

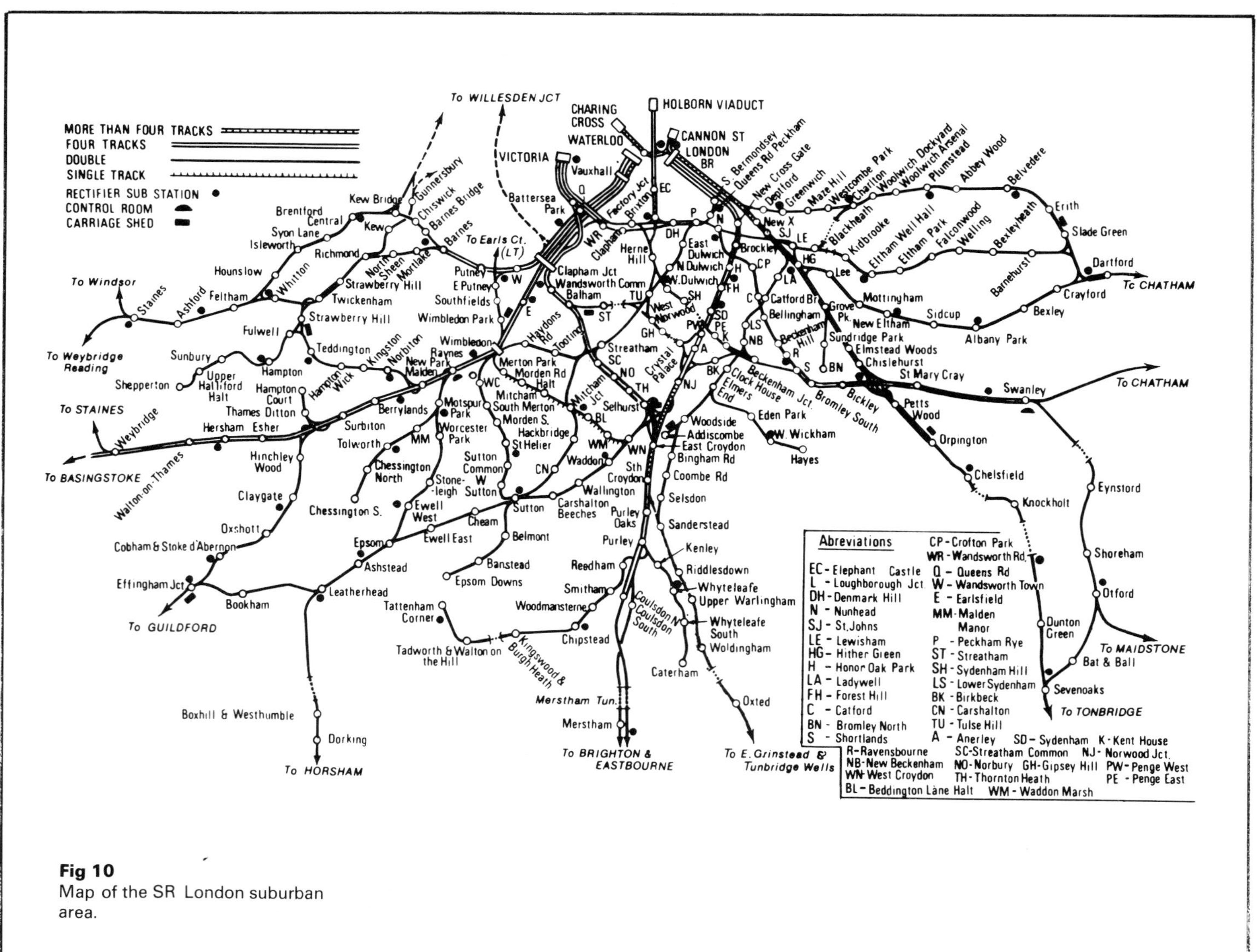

Fig 10
Map of the SR London suburban area.

Bibliography

This bibliography is confined to books and articles centred on the Southern Railway period. Some carry the story on into Southern Region days, some have chapters on the constituent companies. There is, of course, a wealth of literature devoted to the constituents, but if all these had been included the bibliography would have become a handbook in itself.

HISTORY

Allen, Cecil J.; *Salute to the Southern*; Ian Allan Ltd, 1974.

Dendy Marshall, C. F.; *A History of the Southern Railway*; The Southern Railway Company, 1936. Revised by R. W. Kidner and republished in two volumes by Ian Allan Ltd, 1963. Reprinted in a combined volume 1968 and 1982.
This is the classic Southern Railway history, including the constituents. In the first edition the maps were inadequate for so complex a subject but this has been amply rectified in R. W. Kidner's revision, and useful appendices added. They include lists of stations opened and closed, and station name changes.

Gray, Adrian; *The London to Brighton line, 1841-1977*; (Oakwood Library of Railway History No 43) The Oakwood Press 1977.

Kidner, R. W.; *The Southern Railway* (Oakwood Library of Railway History No 56); The Oakwood Press, 1958
(reprinted 1974 with a note on subsequent events).
All the essentials from 1923 in only 52 pages.

Klapper, C. F.; *Sir Herbert Walker's Southern Railway*; Ian Allan Ltd, 1973.
A 'management' history of the Southern focusing on the personality of the General Manager who guided the development of the new Group and the officers who worked with him, many of whom were known personally to the author.

White, H. P.; *Regional History of the railways of Great Britain, Vol 2, Southern England*; David & Charles, 1961.

LOCOMOTIVES AND ROLLING STOCK

Allen, Cecil J. and Townroe, S. C.; *The Bulleid Pacifics of the Southern Railway*; First published Ian Allan Ltd, 1951, reprinted 1977.
Two experts consider these celebrated locomotives in a style intended to be, in their own words, 'neither superficial nor abstruse'.

Bradley D. L.; *Locomotives of the Southern Railway*; Two volumes, Vol 2 in 1977. The Railway Correspondence & Travel Society.
Technical data and detailed records of individual locomotives and duties.

Bulleid, H. A. V.; *Bulleid of the Southern*; Ian Allan Ltd, 1977.
A biography of O. V. S. Bulleid by his son, portraying the man and his individual approach to the problems of the steam locomotive.

Casserley, H. C. and Johnston, S. W.; *Locomotives at the Grouping*; Ian Allan Ltd, 1965.
Brief data on all classes taken into the Southern Railway, with dates of building, number of locomotives in each class, building and withdrawal dates.

Gould, D.; *Bulleid's Steam Passenger Stock*; The Oakwood Press, 1980.

Gould, D.; *Maunsell's Steam Passenger Stock, 1923-1939*; The Oakwood Press, 1978.
These two books give outline descriptions of the various types, with layout plans; vehicle and set numbers; withdrawal dates; and much information on stock workings.

Haresnape, Brian; *Maunsell Locomotives*; Ian Allan Ltd, 1977.
A pictorial history forming a concise and abundantly illustrated review of the Maunsell classes.

Haresnape, Brian; *Bulleid Locomotives*; Ian Allan Ltd, 1977.
Similar in style and presentation to *Maunsell Locomotives*.

Jackman, Michael; *Thirty Years at Bricklayers Arms*; David & Charles, 1976.
Personal reminiscence of Southern Railway classes at the depot during a career which began as a cleaner in 1947.

Kidner, R. W.; *Service Stock of the Southern Railway*; The Oakwood Press, 1980.
A copiously illustrated record.

Kidner, R. W.; *Southern Railway Rolling Stock* ('Locomotion Papers' No 74); The Oakwood Press, 1974.
Concentrates on vehicles taken over from constituent companies. Scaled drawings, photographs.

King, M., Blackburn, A., Bixley, G., Chorley, R., Newton, J.; *An Illustrated History of Southern Wagons* (2 Vol); Oxford Railway Publishing Co.

Nock, O. S.; *Southern Steam*; David & Charles, 1966.
Reviews locomotive practice of the constituent companies as well as the Maunsell and Bulleid eras. Numerous logs of runs.

Nock, O. S. *The Southern 'King Arthur' Family*. David & Charles, 1976.
History and performance of a class with a varied background.

Pallant, N.; *Hither Green Motive Power Depot*; The Oakwood Press, 1980.
Combines history with the 'atmosphere' created by the men and machines based at the depot.

Reeve, G, Hawkins, H.; *An Illustrated History of Southern Sheds 1923-1947*; Oxford Railway Publishing Co, 1979.

Rogers, Col H. C. B.; *Bulleid Pacifics at Work*; Ian Allan, 1980.
An objective record of an interesting venture in design, often regarded as innovatory but perhaps not taking full advantage of some contemporary and proven advances in the steam locomotive.

Townroe, S. C.; *The Arthurs, Nelsons and Schools of the Southern*; Ian Allan Ltd, 1973.
First-hand experience told by an author from the SR Locomotive Running Department.

Winding, Peter F.; 'New Cross'; *Railway World*; December 1978.
'Longhedge'; *Railway World*; February 1980.
'Nine Elms'; *Railway World*; November 1980.
These articles in the author's 'Historic Locomotive Depots' series are often illustrated with his own drawings and paintings, together with pre-Grouping and post-Grouping photographs of locomotives 'on shed', layout diagrams, and locomotive allocation lists.

Winkworth, D. W.; *Bulleid's Pacifics*; George Allen & Unwin, 1974.
Maunsell's 'Nelsons'; George Allen & Unwin, 1981.

ELECTRIFICATION

Cock, C. M.; 'Electric Traction on the Southern Railway', *Proc IEE, Vol 95, Part 2*; pp115-135.
A paper delivered to the Institution of Electrical Engineers on 6 November 1947. See also *The Railway Gazette*, 7 November 1947.

Cooper, B. K.; 'The Southern booster locomotives'; *Railway World*, November 1976.
Principles of the motor-generator system developed for the first Southern Railway electric locomotives and later modified for the BR Class 71 electrics and Class 74 electro-diesels.

Moody, G. T.; *Southern Electric 1909-1979*; Ian Allan Ltd. Fifth edition 1979.
Since 1957 a standard work on the development of the system, its motive power, and train services.

Rayner, B.; 'Pioneer British ac electrification schemes'; *Railway World*, June 1979.
Includes the development and equipment of the LBSC single-phase ac system which continued under Grouping until 1929.

OPERATING AND TRAIN SERVICES

Allen, P. C. and Macleod, A. B.; *Rails in the Isle of Wight*; George Allen & Unwin Ltd; 1967.

Barter, S.; Flying and Burrowing Junctions on the Southern Railway. *The Railway Gazette*, 6 and 13 November 1936.

Bonavia, M. R.; 'The Waterloo & City Railway'; *Railway World*, July 1979.

Casserley, H. C.; *Recollections of the Southern*; D. Bradford Barton Ltd, 1976.
An album with extended captions.

Kidner, R. W.; *Southern Railway branch lines in the Thirties*; The Oakwood Press, 1976.

Webster, V. R.; 'Via Reading'; *Railway World*, March 1979.
Development of services from the West Midlands to the Kent and Sussex coasts via the Reading-Tonbridge line.

Webster, V. R.; 'To the Sunny South'; *Railway World*, October and December 1980.
By-passing London termini by connections with the West London and West London Extension lines.

TOPOGRAPHICAL

Course, Edwin; *The Railways of Southern England: The Main Lines*; B. T. Batsford Ltd, 1973. *The Railways of Southern England: Secondary and Branch Lines*; B. T. Batsford Ltd, 1974.
History, operating details and train services with route descriptions and diagrams.

LIVERIES

Carter, E. F.; *Britain's Railway Liveries*; Burke Publishing Co, 1952 (Third Edition 1980).
A standard work on the subject, with colour chart.

Haresnape, B.; *Railway Liveries: Southern*; Ian Allan Ltd, 1982.

Tavender, L.; *HMRS Livery Register No 3, LSWR and Southern*; Historical Model Railway Society.
Includes diagrams of lettering, etc, and colour code.

MARINE

Veale, E. W. P.; *Gateway to the Continent*; Ian Allan Ltd, 1955.
A short history of the Channel crossing.

ARCHITECTURE

Wikeley, N. and Middleton J.; *Railway Stations — Southern Region*; Peco Publications & Publicity Ltd, 1971.
An experts' illustrated commentary on the architectural styles of the Southern Railway and its predecessors. The illustrations show the stations as they were in the British Rail period.

110
Southern Railway crest; official drawing of revised version produced in 1947. *BR*

Index

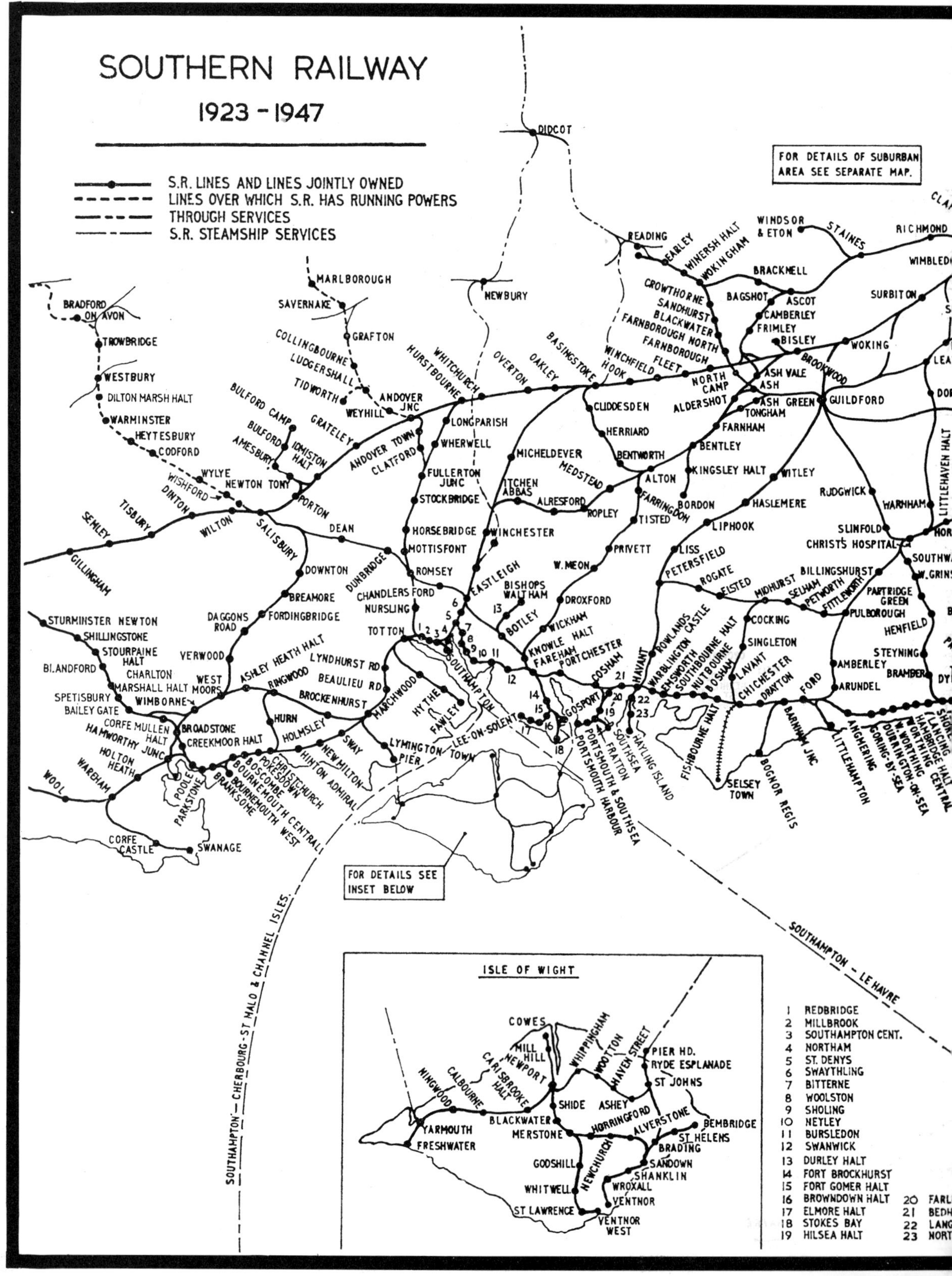

SOUTHERN RAILWAY
1923 - 1947
S.R. LINES AND LINES JOINTLY OWNED
LINES OVER WHICH S.R. HAS RUNNING POWERS
THROUGH SERVICES
S.R. STEAMSHIP SERVICES
FOR DETAILS OF SUBURBAN AREA SEE SEPARATE MAP.
DIDCOT
READING
EARLEY
WINERSH HALT
WOKINGHAM
WINDSOR & ETON
STAINES
RICHMOND
WIMBLED
BRACKNELL
CROWTHORNE
SANDHURST
BLACKWATER
FARNBOROUGH NORTH
FARNBOROUGH
FLEET
BAGSHOT
ASCOT
CAMBERLEY
FRIMLEY
SURBITON
BISLEY
BROOKWOOD
WOKING
NEWBURY
MARLBOROUGH
SAVERNAKE
GRAFTON
COLLINGBOURNE
LUDGERSHALL
TIDWORTH
WEYHILL
ANDOVER JNC
BRADFORD ON AVON
TROWBRIDGE
WESTBURY
DILTON MARSH HALT
WARMINSTER
HEYTESBURY
CODFORD
WYLYE
WISHFORD
NEWTON TONY
BULFORD CAMP
BULFORD
AMESBURY
IDMISTON HALT
GRATELEY
ANDOVER TOWN
CLATFORD
PORTON
DINTON
WILTON
SALISBURY
TISBURY
SEMLEY
GILLINGHAM
HURSTBOURNE
WHITCHURCH
OVERTON
OAKLEY
BASINGSTOKE
HOOK
WINCHFIELD
NORTH CAMP
ASH VALE
ASH
ASH GREEN
ALDERSHOT
TONGHAM
GUILDFORD
FARNHAM
BENTLEY
KINGSLEY HALT
BORDON
WITLEY
HASLEMERE
LIPHOOK
LONGPARISH
WHERWELL
FULLERTON JUNC
STOCKBRIDGE
HORSEBRIDGE
MOTTISFONT
ROMSEY
DUNBRIDGE
DEAN
CLIDDESDEN
HERRIARD
BENTWORTH
MICHELDEVER
MEDSTEAD
ALTON
FARRINGDON
TISTED
ITCHEN ABBAS
ALRESFORD
ROPLEY
WINCHESTER
PRIVETT
RUDGWICK
WARNHAM
LITTLEHAVEN HALT
SLINFOLD
CHRISTS HOSPITAL
LISS
PETERSFIELD
ROGATE
ELSTED
MIDHURST
SELHAM
PETWORTH
FITTLEWORTH
BILLINGSHURST
PULBOROUGH
PARTRIDGE GREEN
HENFIELD
STEYNING
BRAMBER
AMBERLEY
ARUNDEL
DOWNTON
BREAMORE
FORDINGBRIDGE
DAGGONS ROAD
VERWOOD
WEST MOORS
ASHLEY HEATH HALT
RINGWOOD
CHANDLERS FORD
NURSLING
EASTLEIGH
BISHOPS WALTHAM
W. MEON
DROXFORD
WICKHAM
BOTLEY
KNOWLE HALT
FAREHAM
PORTCHESTER
COSHAM
HAVANT
ROWLANDS CASTLE
WARBLINGTON
EMSWORTH
SOUTHBOURNE HALT
NUTBOURNE
BOSHAM
COCKING
SINGLETON
LAVANT
CHICHESTER
DRAYTON
FORD
STURMINSTER NEWTON
SHILLINGSTONE
STOURPAINE HALT
BLANDFORD
CHARLTON MARSHALL HALT
SPETISBURY
BAILEY GATE
WIMBORNE
CORFE MULLEN HALT
HAMWORTHY JUNC
BROADSTONE
CREEKMOOR HALT
HOLTON HEATH
WAREHAM
WOOL
POOLE
PARKSTONE
BRANKSOME
BOURNEMOUTH WEST
BOURNEMOUTH CENTRAL
BOSCOMBE
POKESDOWN
CHRISTCHURCH
HINTON ADMIRAL
NEW MILTON
SWAY
HOLMSLEY
HURN
BROCKENHURST
LYNDHURST RD
BEAULIEU RD
TOTTON
MARCHWOOD
HYTHE
FAWLEY
SOUTHAMPTON
LYMINGTON TOWN
LYMINGTON PIER
LEE-ON-SOLENT
GOSPORT
FRATTON
SOUTHSEA
PORTSMOUTH & SOUTHSEA
PORTSMOUTH HARBOUR
HAYLING ISLAND
FISHBOURNE HALT
SELSEY TOWN
BARNHAM JNC
BOGNOR REGIS
LITTLEHAMPTON
ANGMERING
GORING-BY-SEA
DURRINGTON-ON-SEA
W. WORTHING
WORTHING CENTRAL
LANCING
CORFE CASTLE
SWANAGE
FOR DETAILS SEE INSET BELOW
SOUTHAMPTON — CHERBOURG - ST MALO & CHANNEL ISLES
SOUTHAMPTON - LE HAVRE
ISLE OF WIGHT
COWES
MILL HILL
NEWPORT
WHIPPINGHAM
WOOTTON
HAVEN STREET
PIER HD.
RYDE ESPLANADE
ST JOHNS
CARISBROOKE HALT
CALBOURNE
NINGWOOD
YARMOUTH
FRESHWATER
SHIDE
ASHEY
BLACKWATER
MERSTONE
HORRINGFORD
ALVERSTONE
BEMBRIDGE
ST HELENS
BRADING
SANDOWN
SHANKLIN
GODSHILL
NEWCHURCH
WHITWELL
WROXALL
VENTNOR
ST LAWRENCE
VENTNOR WEST
1 REDBRIDGE
2 MILLBROOK
3 SOUTHAMPTON CENT.
4 NORTHAM
5 ST. DENYS
6 SWAYTHLING
7 BITTERNE
8 WOOLSTON
9 SHOLING
10 NETLEY
11 BURSLEDON
12 SWANWICK
13 DURLEY HALT
14 FORT BROCKHURST
15 FORT GOMER HALT
16 BROWNDOWN HALT
17 ELMORE HALT
18 STOKES BAY
19 HILSEA HALT